# Eastern Hospitals and English Nurses, the Narrative of Twelve Months' Experience in the Hospitals of Kouali and Scutari, by a Lady Volunteer [F.M. Taylor].

Frances Margaret Taylor

**Nabu Public Domain Reprints:**

You are holding a reproduction of an original work published before 1923 that is in the public domain in the United States of America, and possibly other countries. You may freely copy and distribute this work as no entity (individual or corporate) has a copyright on the body of the work. This book may contain prior copyright references, and library stamps (as most of these works were scanned from library copies). These have been scanned and retained as part of the historical artifact.

This book may have occasional imperfections such as missing or blurred pages, poor pictures, errant marks, etc. that were either part of the original artifact, or were introduced by the scanning process. We believe this work is culturally important, and despite the imperfections, have elected to bring it back into print as part of our continuing commitment to the preservation of printed works worldwide. We appreciate your understanding of the imperfections in the preservation process, and hope you enjoy this valuable book.

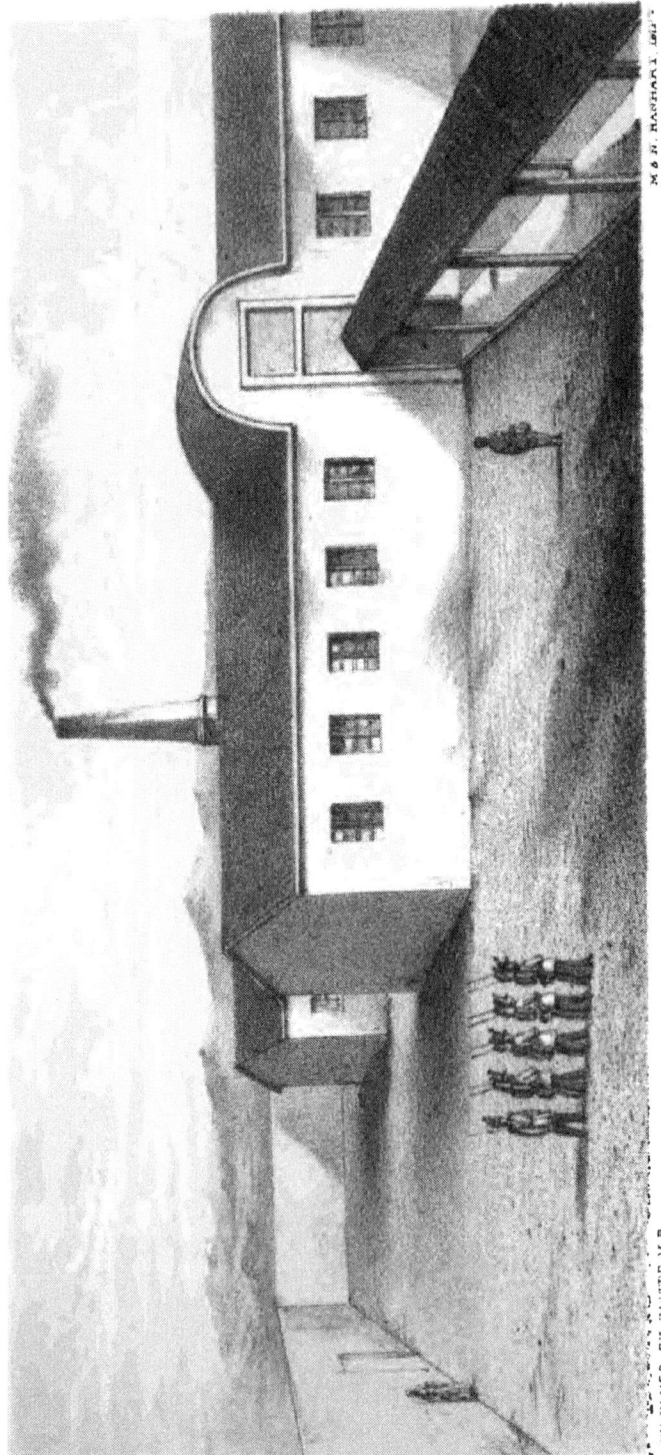

GENERAL HOSPITAL KOULALI.

London, Hurst & Blackett, 1856.

# EASTERN HOSPITALS

AND

# ENGLISH NURSES;

THE NARRATIVE OF

TWELVE MONTHS' EXPERIENCE

IN THE

HOSPITALS OF KOULALI AND SCUTARI.

BY

A LADY VOLUNTEER.

"They are the patient sorrows that touch nearest."—ION.

IN TWO VOLUMES.

VOL. I.

LONDON:
HURST AND BLACKETT, PUBLISHERS,
SUCCESSORS TO HENRY COLBURN,
13, GREAT MARLBOROUGH STREET.
1856.

LONDON: SERCOMBE AND JACK, 16A GREAT WINDMILL STREET.

TO THOSE OF

### The British Army,

WHO DISPLAYED THEIR HEROISM

NOT ONLY ON THE BATTLE FIELD,

BUT IN THE

PATIENT ENDURANCE OF SUFFERING, PRIVATION, AND NEGLECT,

IN THE WARDS OF EASTERN HOSPITALS,

THIS WORK

IS DEDICATED.

## PREFACE.

The deep interest taken by the People of England in all that relates to their army engaged in the Crimean campaign, has been met by innumerable details of the valour of the soldiers on the field, and of their patient endurance amidst the hardships of the siege; but of the heroism displayed by those who suffered in the obscurity of the Hospital Ward, there has been as yet but slight mention made. For this reason one of the band of Englishwomen who went out, and assisted in alleviating the sufferings of the sick and wounded soldiers, ventures on her return to lay before her countrymen some account of the sufferings and the uncomplaining patience of those brave men, and also of the gradual improvements that were subsequently made in the hospitals. And, knowing that very many persons took a deep interest in the proceedings of the nurses, the writer has felt encouraged to add a narrative of their domestic life, and of the perplexities which often beset them, as well as of the pleasing and amusing incidents which occasionally varied the scene. She is indebted to the kindness of some of her companions for many of the anecdotes, as well as for the letters from soldiers who had been under their care; and it is believed that none of the incidents have been overcoloured, as it has been the writer's wish to "nothing extenuate, or aught set down in malice."

*March 30th,* 1856.

# CONTENTS.

### CHAPTER I.

News of the battle of the Alma—French Sisters of Charity—The first application to Miss Nightingale—Party spirit yields to the spirit of charity—Departure of the first band of English nurses—The battles of Balaclava and Inkermann—A summons for more nurses—Formation of a second band—Details of costume—Terms of agreement with the Government . 1 to 15

### CHAPTER II.

The nurses at London Bridge Station—The Boulogne fishwomen—Passage down the Rhone to Valence—Avignon—Marseilles—A stormy night—Stromboli—Messina and its scenery—The Cathedral—A second storm—At anchor off the Piræus—The plains of Troy—*Les Sœurs de la Charité*—The Golden Horn and Constantinople—Extraordinary beauty of the scene—The hospitals—Impatience and disappointment . . . . . . . . . 16 to 35

### CHAPTER III.

Therapia—Evils of the equality system—Christmas-day in Turkey—The Greek church at Therapia—The

Greek service—View from the Giants' Hill—Continued delay at Therapia—Silent bargaining—Atmosphere of the hospitals—Work for the nurses—Intensely cold weather—Alarm of fire—A day of spring—The ward burying-ground—In memoriam—Our superintendent—The faithful wife—A nursing staff for Balaclava—More disappointment—An instance of zeal—A dangerous voyage—The "Melbourne" at last . 36 to 64

## CHAPTER IV.

The establishment at Therapia broken up—Scutari Barrack Hospital—Domestic arrangements—The kitchen—The Ladies' quarters—A sad evening walk—Distribution of the work—Moments of despondency—The diet roll—Serious objections to some of the regulations respecting it—Inefficient state of the purveying department—Miss Nightingale's diet kitchen—The orderly and nurse—The Inspector-General's order respecting cooking in the wards—Military discipline out of season—The General Hospital, Scutari—The British burying ground—The cemetery of the Turks—An unkind orderly—The Valley of the Shadow of Death—Clean linen—Comparative uselessness of the free-gift store—Prevalence of sickness among the nurses—Details of their daily life—Untempered misery—More guests—Those who died and those whom they left behind them—How the story will be told—Letters home . . . 65 to 99

## CHAPTER V.

Koulali—Roads in Turkey—Koulali Barrack Hospital—Peculiar construction of the wards—The Convalescent Hospital—Character of the scenery about Koulali—The General Hospital—The sick from the trenches

—Classification of wards—Hospital diet arrangements—Sickness amongst the nurses . . . . 100 to 110

## CHAPTER VI.

Establishment of an extra-diet kitchen—Rough luxuries—Dismissal of a nurse, and her attempt to commit suicide—Arrival of Irish soldiers at the hospital—Terrible cases of frost-bite—Private Fitzgerald—News of the death of the Russian emperor—An earthquake—The Russian prisoners—Distressing cases of delirium—Zeal and admirable conduct of the Sisters of Mercy . . . . . . . . . 111 to 131

## CHAPTER VI.*

Scenes in the nurses' room—An impertinent orderly—A minor misery—The strange interpreter—The hungry soldier—Miss Smythe's illness—Her death—The grave in a strange land—Miss Stanley's departure for England—Preparations for new arrivals—Change of quarters—Unwearied zeal of the Sisters of Mercy—The "Times" Commissioner—The dangerous person—Longing of the sick for fresh fruit—Mr. Stow's death . . . . . . . . 132 to 151

## CHAPTER VII.

New arrivals—Appointment of a Lady Superintendent—Illness of the last lady of Miss Stanley's band—The "Home" on the Bosphorus—Another earthquake—The plague of rats—The routine of an English nurse's life in an Eastern hospital—Mr. Stow's last visit—Commencement of night-work—Turkish ceremonial and haréem hospitality—Dancing girls . 152 to 173

## CHAPTER VIII.

Arrangement of the wards—Details of management—The jarring question—Better times—Gratitude of the

CONTENTS.

patients—The drummer-boy—Yearnings for home—The old age of sickness—Our orderlies—A case of "delirium tremens"—The gentleman private—The English village-boy in an Eastern hospital—A last will and testament—The reformed corporal . . 174 to 197

## CHAPTER IX.

The youth of the patients—An eccentric character—The general's visit—An idle ward-master—Care and tenderness—The Italian patient—The little sailor—Good advice—Letters home—The affectionate wife—Lower stable ward—Its arrangements—A member of the Evangelical Alliance—A case of frost-bite—The kind doctor—The sick man's home sickness—Cases in the upper division of stable ward—Sergeant Everett—Another case of *delirium tremens*—False newspaper paragraphs—Russian prisoners—Kindness of the patients towards each other—Newspaper reading in the hospital—Men dressmakers—The untaught artist—A new Shelley—Cat and kitten—An instance of patience . . 198 to 225

## CHAPTER X.

No. 4 ward—Sister Anne—The fever patient—A case of delirium—A terrible cholera case—The convalescent's relapse—Bitter tears—The pain of gratitude—Habits of drinking overcome—A sergeant's letter—Goody—His kindness and attention to the patients—The surly orderly—A ward-master under arrest—Fortune out of misfortune—Letters to Sister Anne . . . . . . . 226 to 246

## CHAPTER XI.

No. — Upper Ward—Civil and Military Surgeons—Dr. —— and his experiments—His advice to the

CONTENTS. xi

PAGES

nurses—The starving system—Miserable state of No. —Ward—An instance of Dr. ——'s eccentricity —Milk in Turkey—Short allowance—The sick boy on the banks of the Bosphorus—Dick and Algeon—The facetious orderly . . . . . 247 to 257

## CHAPTER XII.

The General Hospital at Koulali—Tradition respecting its site—The Turks' plan of building their hospitals—Dr. Hamilton—Nursing arrangements of the General Hospital at Koulali—Insufficiency of the Sisters' quarters—Their community-room—The Sisters' happiness in their work—The consumptive patient—Sugar-plums in the East—Great treasures in small things—Prevalence of chronic rheumatism—A private soldier's history—The large-hearted Irishman—A quiet cure—Convalescent yearnings for country rambles—The Sisters' influence over the soldiers—Vehement gratitude of the Irish—The Convalescent Ward—No nurses required for it—Afternoon visits—Its admirable state of order . . . . . . . . . . 258 to 275

## CHAPTER XIII.

Nightwork—Its origin—Its necessity—Sleepy orderlies—" All's well "—Drowsy sentinels—Our fellow watchers—Wood gathering—Gratitude of the Russian prisoners for a cup of tea—Heart-breaking work—The restlessness of cholera patients—A cheerful Scotchman—The long, long night—Violent storms—Danger of being shot as felonious Greeks—The fair light of dawn . . . . 276 to 290

## CHAPTER XIV.

Shopping at Pera—An amusing half-hour's voyage—A miscellaneous crowd—Conversations with Turkish ladies—The beauty of the Bosphorus—The Sultan's lilac-coloured palace—The Sultan's usual residence—A marble mosque—Vicus Michaelicus—The principal French Military hospital—Galata and Tophani—The Frank quarter—Scene of a massacre in the reign of Constantine—Constantine and his brothers—The tower of Galata—Liberality of the Greek emperors towards the Genoese—A street scene in Galata—Turkish porters—Swarms of beggars in Constantinople—A climb up the hill of Pera—The Hotel d'Angleterre—The Russian and Dutch embassies—The shops in the Grande Rue—Ideas of the Turkish shopkeepers in respect to English wealth—Picturesque bustle in the Grande Rue—The British embassy—A funeral procession—Death crowned with roses—Caiques and Caidjees—A row on the Bosphorus—"Sooltan, Sooltan"—Turkish Court etiquette—Sunset. . . 291 to 31

## CHAPTER XV.

Difficulties attending shopping in Pera—*Sœur* Bernardine—Affection of the French troops for their *Sœurs*—More than sufficient reasons for it—A visit to *La Maison Notre Dame de la Providence*—Extraordinary scene within—Details of its arrangements—Schools connected with it—Church belonging to the Lazaristes Fathers—The orphans' dormitory—Boarding-school under the direction of the *Sœurs*—The children's chapel—A glorious panorama—Founder of the Order of the *Sœurs de la Charité*—Rules of the Order—Extension of the Order to other lands—Voltaire's opinion of it—Foundation of the Mission of the *Sœurs de la Charité* in Constantinople—Sweet *Sœur* Bernardine . . . 314 to 328

# EASTERN HOSPITALS
## AND
# ENGLISH NURSES.

## CHAPTER I.

News of the battle of the Alma—French Sisters of Charity—The first application to Miss Nightingale—Party spirit yields to the spirit of charity—Departure of the first band of English nurses—The battles of Balaclava and Inkermann—A summons for more nurses—Formation of a second band—Details of costume—Terms of agreement with the Government.

THERE are few who will not remember the intense excitement which was roused in England when the newspapers of October 1st announced the battle of Alma—many anxious hopes and fears had been with the army since it left England in March. But months had passed away, little had been done, and expectation had almost ceased when, like the blast of a trumpet, the news of battle and victory rang through the land.

The first burst of exultation had hardly passed away when the lists of killed and wounded arrived, and then the realities of war were brought to almost every English home. The "Gazette" office in London was crowded with inquirers pale with anxiety, who grasped the printed list with trembling hands, and it needed no words to tell the tale revealed to each by the absence or presence of the well-known name in the fatal column. The "Telegraph" office was crowded by friends anxious to convey glad tidings to country homes. All who had letters hastened to communicate their contents to those who had none. The common bond of sympathy spread through the land;

England was like one great family. The lists were followed by the harrowing details of the battle field, the embarkation of the wounded, and their arrival at the imperfectly prepared hospital at Scutari.

These are too well known to need repetition here; the newspapers were filled with complaints, and their statements produced the same effect everywhere. The first cry was that the wounded had arrived and there was no lint or linen to dress their wounds with. The papers were instantly filled with letters offering both—from house to house, parish to parish, lint was collected in bales and tons till the public were assured on official authority that a further supply was not needed.

But the lint letters were succeeded by others, stating a grave deficiency. Nurses were needed—the medical men were overtaxed; the orderlies were ill-accustomed to attend in sickness. Why were the English soldiers to be deprived of the comforts enjoyed by the French? On the first appearance of sickness at Varna they had sent for Sisters of Charity, and the summons was instantly obeyed, and in bands of twenty-five they went as they were wanted. Why, it was said, are there no such nurses in England? Surely there are women in England as well as in France who would go forth and minister to the wants of the sick and wounded soldiers! And English women were not wanting. Many was the band that was that week organised for the work; many were the individuals who in their secluded homes determined to offer their services for this purpose, and applied for information and permission to the official authorities.

Amongst other volunteers was the widowed daughter of an Irish nobleman, Lady M—— F——. She engaged three nurses, furnished money for their outfit and expenses, and on the 11th of October she went to Miss

Nightingale, then in Harley Street, and requested her to take them out to the East, or to recommend some one else, failing which she was ready to go herself! Subject to the approval of her parents—which was given—Miss Nightingale consented to go, and every preparation was made for her departure on the 17th. Her letter to Mr. Sidney Herbert —asking for government protection—was crossed by one from him, earnestly requesting her to undertake the cause and select her own band.

The scheme from this moment became a public one, and though every day's delay was to be deprecated, it was thought desirable to attempt to procure a larger staff of nurses, and therefore Miss Nightingale's departure was delayed for some days. She appointed two ladies to assist her in the selection of nurses, and while they dealt with individuals she dealt with institutions and communities. From the beginning it was determined that all party feeling was to be merged in the one common bond of alleviating suffering, and in the selection of nurses few questions were asked, and no objections made on the ground of differences of creed or shades of opinion.

The only point on which any stress was laid—and it was laid equally on all—was that proselytising was strictly forbidden.

The Master of St. John's House, Westminster, applied to the Bishop of London, on the 13th, saying he was ready to go out and take seven nurses. The Catholic Bishop of Southwark made a similar application to the War-office on the same day, having completed arrangements for five Sisters of Mercy to start immediately, which they did, but were stopped in Paris, and desired to wait for the whole band, which was then organising under Miss Nightingale. All were to be subject to her in matters relating to the hospital. With the approval of the Catholic Bishop of Southwark, rules were issued to the Sisters of Mercy for this special service, the first of which was that the sisters should attend to the corporeal wants of the soldiers, but that they should never introduce religious subjects except with patients of their own faith. The Master of St. John's House accepted Miss Nightingale's terms, after two days consideration.

The institution founded by Mrs. Fry was the first to which Miss Nightingale applied, laying before the Lady Superintendent the terms offered by government; *i. e.* their not being for the time in connection with any other institution. She replied that none of the nurses would consent to go under such conditions, and the proposal therefore at once fell to the ground. Miss Sellon applied towards the middle of this week, and Miss Nightingale consented to take out eight of her sisters.

Between sixty and seventy nurses applied

to go out—owing to the active kindness of friends who searched London for the purpose. Out of this number eleven were selected with great difficulty, owing to the very low calibre of the applicants. By Saturday, October 21st, the band was completed as follows: Ten Catholic Sisters of Mercy; eight of Miss Sellon's sisters; six nurses from St. John's; three selected by Lady M. F——; eleven selected from applicants: total, 38. The only additions were Mr. and Mrs. Bracebridge, who most kindly, at the last moment, offered to go and assist Miss Nightingale. It was on Monday, October 24th, 1854, that this expedition left England, under the escort of Mr. and Mrs. Bracebridge. At Boulogne they were met on landing by the fishwomen, who, hearing their mission, insisted on carrying their luggage, gratis, to the Hotel des Bains, where the landlord provided a sumptuous luncheon for the whole party, for which neither he nor any one in his establishment would accept any remuneration; and he repeated his liberality on the succeeding occasions when bands of nurses passed through on their way to the East.

They proceeded to Marseilles, where the "Vectis" awaited them, and conveyed them, after a stormy passage, to Constantinople, which they reached Saturday, November 4th, and were at once allotted the quarters in the barrack hospital at Scutari which have been thus occupied ever since. Meantime the selection of nurses for future bands was left in the hands of Mrs. Sidney Herbert, Miss Stanley, and Miss Jones, Superintendent of St. John's House, Westminster. Each post, each hour, brought fresh applicants; and, as a test of the qualifications of the applicants, it was agreed that, with few exceptions, all should go through training at some of the London Hospitals, and, to facilitate this, St. John's House and St. Saviour's Home, Osnaburgh Street, were opened to receive probationers, and latterly a third institution was established for the same purpose, under the patronage of the Earl of Shaftesbury, in Charlotte Street, Fitzroy Square.

Tidings from the East were eagerly looked for. At last they came. The nurses had arrived and been well received; and letters were seen from soldiers, from medical men, from military men, all speaking in grateful terms of what women's care already was and would be to them. Many comforts were said to be wanting, and English hearts and English purses were opened to remedy the deficiencies.

The battles of Balaclava and Inkermann sent down hundreds of sufferers. The medical men in England said the numbers of nurses already gone were but as a drop in the ocean amidst the thousands now in the Eastern hospitals; a second band was to be in readiness to go if sent for. The summons came in a letter from Mr. Bracebridge to Mr.

Herbert, who, anxious that as many as possible should benefit by the care of nurses, determined to send out as large a staff as were ready. With as much care as was possible, a selection was made from the registered candidates. Nine ladies and twenty-two paid nurses were chosen; fifteen Catholic Sisters of Mercy, collected from various convents, under the charge of the superioress of the Convent of Kinsale, placed themselves at the service of the Government, and thus the party was composed. Miss Stanley was requested to go out in charge of them, and place them under Miss Nightingale's care, after which it was her intention to return home. The Honourable Mr. Percy and Dr. Meyer were to accompany them to make arrangements.

On December 1st the party of nurses and ladies assembled at Mr. Sidney Herbert's house in Belgrave Square, and the scene which presented itself was extraordinary;

the rooms on the ground floor were turned into a fair, and that not a fancy one—boxes of all sizes, goloshes, cloaks, bonnets, jackets, gowns, collars, caps, lay in admired confusion in all directions. In one room one group were choosing their dresses, and of course short people got long ones, and *vice versâ.*

I had better here describe our "Costume." It consisted of a loose wrapping gown of dark grey tweed, a worsted jacket, plain linen collar, and thick white cap; passing over the right shoulder was a broad strip of brown Holland, embroidered in red worsted with the words "Scutari Hospital." A short grey worsted cloak, brown straw bonnet, and veil, completed the dress.

The party were now summoned to stand in a circle to be addressed by Mr. Sidney Herbert. He told us how useful Miss Nightingale and her party were then making themselves in the hospital; he warned us to expect many hardships and discomforts, and to be prepared to witness many scenes of horror; he impressed upon us the necessity of strict obedience to our superiors, and begged us to remember that we all went out on the same footing as hospital nurses, and that no one was to consider herself as in any way above her companions.

We were now summoned by Mrs. Sidney Herbert to sign our agreement, of which the following is a copy:—"Memorandum of agreement made this 1st day of December 1854, between Miss Nightingale, under the principal medical-officer at ———, on the one part, and ——— of ——— on the other part. Female nurses being required for the sick and wounded of the British Army serving in the East, the Secretary-at-War has agreed to employ the said ——— in the capacity of nurse at a weekly salary of ———, and also to provide board and lodging; also to pay all expenses attendant upon the journeying to or from the present or any future hospital that may be appointed for the accommodation of the sick and wounded of the said army; and to pay all expenses of return to this country, should sickness render it necessary for the said ——— to return, save and except such return shall be rendered necessary by the discharge of the said ——— for neglect of duty, immoral conduct, or intoxication, in which case the said ——— shall forfeit all claim upon the said Miss Nightingale from the period of such discharge. And the said ——— hereby agrees to devote her whole time and attention to the purposes aforesaid, under the directions and to the satisfaction of the said Miss Nightingale, the whole of whose orders she undertakes to obey, until discharged by the said Miss Nightingale. Witness ———, December 1st, 1854."

In the case of volunteers, the sentence respecting payment in the agreement was erased.

The last evening was come. Few of those

concerned in the morrow's departure slept that night. Last things were to be packed, last words spoken, and ere these were finished it was time to prepare for departure.

## CHAPTER II.

The nurses at London Bridge Station—Sympathy of the Boulogne fishwomen—Passage down the Rhone to Valence—Avignon—Marseilles—A stormy night—Stromboli—Messina and its scenery—The Cathedral—A second Storm—At anchor off the Piræus—The plains of Troy—*Les Sœurs de la Charité*—The Golden Horn and Constantinople—Extraordinary beauty of the scene—The hospitals—Impatience and disappointment.

LONG before dawn on that dark December morning, cabs might have been seen in the silent empty streets, all converging to one point, the London Bridge Station. In the large waiting room at the station the singular party assembled all in costume, and attended by innumerable friends, and when the long train of fifteen nuns, in their black serge dresses, white coifs, and long black veils, joined the party, we formed a group such as was never before seen in London Bridge Station.

Mrs. Sidney Herbert, with thoughtful kindness, brought last gifts and encouraging words to cheer all on their way. Gentlemen perambulated the room with "Illustrated News," "Punches," and table-spoons, which latter article seemed to be the last thought for our comfort. We had been informed that whatever luggage we required besides our one box each (which we were never to open from London to Constantinople) we must carry in our hands, consequently we were literally sinking beneath the weight of cloaks, shawls, railway wrappers, baskets, and carpet bags, so that when the cry, "Nurses for Scutari, move on," came, it was with difficulty that many obeyed the summons.

We started about six, heartily cheered by the kind friends who had come to bid us good-bye. We reached Folkestone in two hours, and went straight on board the steamer for Boulogne. It was a lovely morning for the time of year, and Old England's white cliffs stood out brightly in the morning light to receive our looks of farewell. We had a quick but very rough passage, which, with its attendant miseries, there is no need to describe. At Boulogne we were received by the fishwomen, who insisted upon carrying our luggage from the boat to the station. An excellent luncheon was kindly provided for us at the Hotel des Bains, after which we immediately left for Paris, which we reached late at night. Sunday was spent at Paris without incident. Monday we travelled to Lyons. December the 5th, early in the morning, we went on board the steamer to go down the Rhone to Valence. A dense fog came on almost immediately after we went on board, in which the steamer ran aground, and delayed us two hours.

When we were once more on our way the

fog cleared, and the day proved lovely; we greatly enjoyed our voyage down the many windings of the beautiful river. The Alps in the distance were clearly to be seen. We reached Valence in the afternoon; found, as we expected, that our morning delay had caused us to lose the express train to Marseilles, resolved to proceed by the next train to Avignon, and telegraphed to the hotel there that fifty beds should be prepared. We heard afterwards that the hotel-keeper looked upon it as a hoax; however, he discovered his mistake when the fifty actually arrived.

The hotel was a very old-fashioned one, and the windows of our room looked into a dark and narrow street, so narrow that the houses almost seemed to meet. It was a fête-day, and the peasants were dancing by torchlight, and beautiful was the effect of the dark shadows of the houses, and the brilliant glare of light falling on the picturesque dresses of the peasants of Provence.

As we had only to proceed next day to Marseilles, some of our party by rising early managed to visit the Cathedral. It is handsome, but very small in comparison of many in England. It stands in a fine situation, and we were told commands a beautiful view. The pouring rain hid this from our eyes. We arrived at Marseilles at noon, and proceeded to the Hotel d'Europe. There was much to be done at Marseilles by those escorting the party; bed and bedding had to be bought and packed, and taken on board ship. The arrangements for the journey through France were made with the utmost liberality, and were carried out with the greatest consideration for the comfort of the party.

At Marseilles the English consul and chaplain were prompt in their offers to render any assistance in their power, and all through France the officials had been most courteous and attentive. We went out shopping for "last thoughts" in spite of the rain, and visited the flower market, which looked as lovely as if it had been summer.

The astonishment of the paid nurses at the *tables d'hôte* used to be our amusement through France. Their views on the subject of French cookery and French customs were not very favourable. "I don't see the use of just eating one thing by itself, and then eating another by itself," says one; "now I likes two or three of them together." "Yes," we replied, "but that is not the custom in France." "Well, I means to manage it somehow," says another; "I am a-going to keep this ere fowl on my plate till I get some of that cauliflower," and so she did, in spite of the astonished look of the *garçons*, who had, however, made up their minds that they were a set of wild animals, from whom anything might have been expected.

It was in the afternoon of December the 7th that the party embarked in the "Egyptus," one of the French mail steamers. She was carrying between two and three hundred French soldiers and officers to the seat of war, and was consequently very much crowded. The nurses expressed great dissatisfaction when they first saw their accommodation in the fore-cabin. The Sisters of Mercy were offered a share of first-class berths, but declined them, preferring to be all together in two of the fore-cabins. The ladies were all in saloon cabins.

The very first night was stormy, and it appeared the "Egyptus" was out of repair; and but for the great demand for troop ships she would have been in the docks six months before. Her decks required caulking, and nothing was secure. Press of weather drove the "Egyptus" into Hyeres for some hours. Towards evening of the 8th the gale went down, and we proceeded on our way. The French soldiers all slept on deck, and they used to go to sleep at dusk; so after dinner, the favourite time on board ship for taking a walk, one could not pace five yards without stumbling upon a Frenchman wrapped in his grey coat: he never seemed to mind it or even to wake. A miserable-looking set of boys were those poor French soldiers.

We had rather rough weather until the night of December 11th, when the sea became quite calm, and not long after midnight the announcement was made that we were passing Stromboli. Many of us went on deck. We passed close by the island, which is like a rock glowing with fire in the midst of the ocean. Every now and then a bright flame burst out, blazed for a moment, and then disappeared; and then the rock glowed again so intensely as if it would almost burn and consume itself; and yet there it has burnt from age to age, and will still burn on.

At daylight we anchored off Messina; and after some delay, before we found out there was no quarantine, most of us went on shore. The Sisters of Mercy remained on board—they considered it contrary to their rule to leave the vessel except on business.

Great was the enjoyment of that day. Winter seemed to have vanished. It was like the loveliest summer's day, so bright, and fresh, and sweet. Groves loaded with oranges and lemons, the bright blue Mediterranean calm as a lake, the mountains of Calabria in the distance, and the picturesque town of Messina itself,—all this lay spread before us as we stood on the steps of the church of San Angelo.

We went into the church, and there the beauty of art tried hard to rival that of nature. The church is very small; but the interior is entirely of mosaic, in excellent preservation; the roof fresco. It was a spot in which one could have spent hours in delight and wonder at its marvellous beauty; but our time of course was short. We went further up the hill, to the Capuchin monastery, into the garden of which the gentlemen of our party were admitted, and they brought from it handsful of oranges, given by the good monks to comfort the ladies for not being permitted to enter. We saw their chapel, however, which was poor and small.

Descending the hill into the town, we visited the Cathedral. Over the west door is a most beautiful piece of sculpture. Over the high altar is a small picture of the Madonna and Child, believed to have been painted by St. Luke, and accordingly preserved in a silver case, set with precious stones; so carefully preserved is it that we could hardly see the picture. The archbishop's throne was hung with Tyrian purple, what we should call a very pale lilac. Leaving the cathedral, we walked through the streets to regain the shore. They were filthy beyond description. It is said to be the dirtiest continental town; but even the dirt does not take off the picturesque effect. The very tall white houses, with draperies of the brightest colours hanging out of the windows; the shops, also hanging out their goods of various hues; the costume of the people, and the glimpses as we turned down every strada of the lovely bay, made our walk through Messina a delightful one.

Towards evening we went on board, and soon after sailed. A second storm occurred after leaving Messina, and a terrible night and day followed. For those who never moved from their berths, in the saloon cabins it did not much signify, but the unhappy occupants of fore-cabins were far worse off. In the middle of the night the skylight was torn off, and the sea poured into the cabins occupied by the nuns and nurses. The nurses on this occasion behaved extremely well, no murmurs escaped their lips. Gratefully they received every attempt to better their condition; and the ensuing night, of their own accord, they offered up a thanksgiving to Almighty God for their safe deliverance from the perils of the storm.

The scene of the storm was past description, the men darted in to bale out the water, some were too sick to care for anything, some called "*garçon*," and others began to prepare for instant death. When daylight came the poor sisters found that the sea had penetrated into their trunks; and books and clothes, and ornaments for their chapel, were entirely spoiled. The misery the poor sisters endured, and most patiently, during this voyage was untold. No breakfast could be got that day; so sick and well fasted till dinner time, when the storm began to abate, and the night of December the 11th was spent in the harbour of Navarino.

On December the 15th we anchored off the Piræus; great delay was caused by our getting on shore, owing to quarantine having been established for cholera some time back.

It did not, however, then exist, so we landed at last, with peremptory orders from the captain to be on board again by noon.

Upon landing, we found it would be out of the question to visit Athens, which is a distance of six miles from the Piræus. We contented ourselves with driving about the green hills and gazing on the distant view. We returned on board at noon; but the despatches for which the captain was obliged to wait did not come till 4 P.M., so that we might have gone to Athens after all. We had good weather after leaving the Piræus; Saturday, December the 16th, we passed the plains of Troy, one evening at sunset (they were covered with indescribably lovely tints of soft lilac: that is the only expression which seems to describe it, but it was a colour rarely if ever seen before), and entered the Dardanelles.

It was dark before we reached Gallipoli, where we anchored for some hours. Two

French *Sœurs de la Charité* came on board to proceed to Constantinople. Many of us had never seen *les Sœurs de la Charité* before; we found on inquiry that they belonged to the order of St. Vincent de Paul, and are bound only by annual vows. The order was founded two hundred years ago, and they wear the peasant dress of that period, consisting of grey serge, with jacket and loose sleeves, and a large stiff white peasant cap, of which it is said one of the kings of France invented the shape by folding his dinner napkin into it.

The ship was so crowded that there was not a single berth for the *sœurs*, and they were quite contented to sit up all night, but they received a warm welcome from the Sisters of Mercy, who invited them to share their small cabin for the night. Next morning some of our party who could converse in French were anxious to talk to them, but they were prevented. The French officers and soldiers on board evidently looked upon *les sœurs* as their exclusive property, and treated them with affectionate respect; immediately they made their appearance on deck they were surrounded by their countrymen, who did not relinquish them until we arrived at our destination. The last day of voyage had arrived; Sunday the 17th found the "Egyptus" rolling through the Sea of Marmora.

About noon the first haze of Constantinople appeared on the horizon, and every eye was fixed in that direction. The first distant view disappointed us. But it is only on rounding Seraglio Point, and entering the Golden Horn, that, as the eye slowly gathers in the wonderful extent of mosques and minarets, the varied shipping, the palaces and the groves of cypresses, the marvellous beauty of the imperial city bursts forth. No travellers had before, we supposed, so quickly called off their attention from the beautiful panorama of Constantinople, to gaze on objects which, though possessing no beauty, were full of interest to them—the hospitals of Scutari, the goal of their long travel, and our future home. Both stand in commanding positions near the edge of the cliff overhanging the Sea of Marmora, looking upon the Golden Horn, Seraglio Point, and the city in the distance; how our hearts burned and yearned to be in those hospitals, to be accomplishing the object for which we had left our dear country and our loved homes, to be soothing in some small degree a portion of the mighty mass of suffering collected in those wards. Such were our thoughts as we slowly passed Scutari and anchored in the Golden Horn.

The vast collection of shipping which fills the bay adds greatly to the extraordinary beauty of the scene. At this time the flags of all nations except the Russian were flying. The fairy-like caiques shot rapidly by (even the commonest of these boats were richly ornamented with carving); then came the pasha's caiques with their bright cushions and carpets, their six rowers all dressed in white with the crimson fez, the pasha himself sitting in state with his pipe-bearer behind him; then came the heavy passage boats loaded with passengers and luggage, among the former, numbers of Turkish women closely wrapped in their feridgee and yachmac; the rowers of these passage boats rise from their seats each time they raise their oar, so that their progress is slow and tedious. These were some of the strange sights we watched that Sunday afternoon from the deck of the "Egyptus."

One of the gentlemen of our escort went in a caique to Scutari to announce our arrival to Miss Nightingale. All agreed it was necessary we should sleep on board that night. The passengers who were not of our party soon went on shore, while we sat watching the sunset as its golden light fell upon tower and minaret, and shed a sort of halo over the queenly city. We watched till the stars came out; then the moon rose, and beautiful indeed looked Constantinople bathed in its soft silver rays.

Mr. Bracebridge came on board that evening and brought news that the next morning the admiral's small steamer would be alongside to convey us, not to Scutari, but to a house belonging to the ambassador at Therapia—a village fifteen miles up the Bosphorus, on the European side—the reason of this change being that there was no room for us at present at Scutari.

This news insensibly cast a damp over our spirits, although it seemed but reasonable that we should be delayed for a few days. The French Sisters of Charity, who have a large convent in Galata, sent to offer to receive the Sisters of Mercy for a short time, for, it being the Christmas holidays, and their boarding-school having broken up, they were enabled to spare them a room in their generally well-crowded convent.

As we all looked forward to a week's delay as the longest possible time, this offer was accepted, and next morning the party separated. The nuns proceeded to Galata, the ladies and nurses, under Miss Stanley's charge, to Therapia, the gentlemen to an hotel in Pera. On December the 18th, with thankful hearts for our merciful preservation through a perilous voyage, we quitted the "Egyptus," and the little steamer quickly conveyed us to Therapia. It was a pleasant passage; the banks of the Bosphorus are thickly crowded with houses, which often overhang the waters. Here and there a small Turkish cemetery, with its dark cypresses and gaily-coloured tombstones, or a Sultan's palace, with its terraced gardens, or mosques and minarets of snowy whiteness, diversify the scene; on the high points of the hills, are the picturesque kiosks, or summer houses, the many windings of the Bosphorus, the dark hills and valleys between, the varied colouring of the wooden houses on either side, made our passage up to Therapia seem like a series of pictures.

## CHAPTER III.

Therapia—Evils of the equality system—Christmas-day in Turkey—The Greek Church at Therapia—The Greek service—View from the Giant's Hill—Continued delay at Therapia—Silent bargaining—Atmosphere of the hospitals—Work for the nurses—Intensely cold weather—Alarm of fire—A day of spring—The Naval burying-ground—In memoriam—Our superintendent—The faithful wife—A nursing staff for Balaclava—More disappointment—An instance of zeal—A dangerous voyage—The "Melbourne" at last.

WE reached Therapia about eleven in the morning, and the steamer anchored at the quay immediately before the house we were to occupy, which was the summer residence of the *attachés* of the British embassy. The quay, which divides the house from the Bosphorus, is about four yards wide. Entering the garden and ascending a long flight of steps led us into a long hall, from which various rooms opened. All the rooms in the house were on this floor; the kitchen, as in most Turkish houses, separate from the house. The house was only partially furnished, but all deficiencies were supplied that afternoon from Constantinople, and the evening was spent in arrangements.

Miss Stanley refused assistance from the English hotel in Therapia, thinking it best to employ the paid nurses in the household work which was to be performed. But now the evils of the equality system began to appear. The ladies had suffered by it through the journey, for having no authority to restrain the hired nurses they were compelled to listen to the worst language, and to be treated not unfrequently with coarse insolence. Whispers were heard amongst them that first evening, that they had come out to nurse the soldiers and not to sweep, wash, and cook.

that it would be a very warm situation in summer were it not for the breezes from the Black Sea, which render it the most delightful atmosphere in Turkey.

Around the house in which we lived was a large garden, at the extreme end of which, quite hidden among the trees, was a small house, the summer residence of Lord Napier, Secretary to the Embassy; the use of this house also was offered to us by Lord Stratford de Redcliffe, and it was assigned by Miss Stanley for the use of the nuns, after they had been a few days at Galata. After passing the Hotel d'Angleterre the stone quay ends, and the village begins, which consists of a few wretched shops, some *cafés*, a French *magasin*, and a small Greek church.

After passing through the village the quay recommences, there are a few better sort of houses, then two large buildings, which were at that time converted into

British and French naval hospitals, and the Sultan's palace: eventually this last became the British naval convalescent hospital, but at the time we were at Therapia they possessed only the one building.

On Christmas-day there was no English service. The chaplain being indisposed, prayers were read at home, and we adorned the rooms with green, sang carols, and tried to make ourselves believe it was really Christmas-day. Lady Stratford, with her well-known kindness, sent up mince pies and plum-pudding, with kind Christmas wishes. We were very grateful for her kind remembrance of us, but our Christmas was a dreary one. The joyous sounds of English Christmases were ringing in our ears, and it was an oppressive thought to remember that through the length and breadth of that fair land, save from the few bodies of strangers who dwelt in it for a time, there went up no sounds of rejoicing for the glad tidings of great joy. No bells rang out to welcome the birthday of the King of kings.*

Therapia is quite a Greek village. The services at the Greek church are most curious and picturesque. The church itself is small and common-looking outside, inside much decorated with pictures, chandeliers, great candlesticks, aud painted pillars, all rather tawdry when looked into except the rood screen, which is one of the most beautiful pieces of carving I ever beheld; it reaches entirely to the ceiling, and it is only in the space above the door which admits the priest into the chancel that you catch a view of the altar. This space is generally covered with an embroidered curtain only withdrawn at mass. The service was most extraordinary. Two priests stood in stalls in the nave with large books, out of which they chanted (at least I suppose it was intended

* The Greek Church celebrates Christmas twelve days later.

for such), but it sounded like the most dismal howling. It was an indescribably discordant noise. The congregation employed themselves in walking up to two or three little pictures and kissing them repeatedly. They then crossed themselves a great many times, and lighted the smallest wax tapers in the world, which they stuck by the side of the same little pictures. Then the curtain before the altar was drawn back, and the priest appeared in an under robe of dark brown and fur, and an outer one of crimson and gold. He was an old man, with a long white beard. He brought with him a censer, with which he incensed the people, then the host was carried round the church, the people forming into two lines as it passed, the men bowing the head, the women bending down till their hands touched the ground—they never kneel. We could not understand the service; it did not seem like the celebration of mass. The priest at the altar was saying prayers, but the two in the nave would not let his voice be heard: they continued their musical sounds so as to drown all others.

It was certainly a most striking scene. The Greek men are a handsome race, very different to the women, who are extremely plain; even the commonest race of men are all like pictures—the dress doubtless has something to do with it. On Sundays and *fête*-days it is so picturesque; the full trousers gathered in at the knee, the tunic of the same colour, perhaps of deep blue, showing the embroidered vest, the bright-coloured scarf round the waist, and the crimson fez. Nothing can equal getting through the streets of Constantinople at this season. The way of walking is for each to hold by the other's cloak, and to walk in a string; what with the musk and the constant danger of being run over, walking in Constantinople is rather a laborious occupation.

Some of our party took an excursion to the Giant's Hill, on the Asiatic shore. It is the highest point of the hills of the Bosphorus, and from its summit there is a fine view of the Black Sea, the Golden Horn, and the Sea of Marmora. When they were all safe at home again they were told they might have been carried off by the Bashi Bazouks, and kept till they were ransomed! Our readers may believe this as they please.

Our life flowed on monotonously enough at Therapia,—ironing the clothes which the nurses condescended to wash for us, taking a walk on the quay when weather permitted, and writing home, were the employments day after day. How long the weeks seemed! The constant expectation contributed to heighten this feeling. Every Sunday we hoped the next would see us at work, and Sunday after Sunday brought disappointment.

Miss Stanley answered all our inquiries as to the delay by stating that, in consequence of the arrival of eight hundred sick from the camp, there was no room for us at Scutari, and we were to remain where we were till arrangements were made for our employment.

The occasional amusement to some of us was shopping. We not understanding a word of Greek, and the shopkeepers knowing no English, the bargain was conducted entirely by signs; for instance, the supply of flat irons being very insufficient, one of the party volunteered to buy one; every one said she would never find it. She resolved to try, so she pointed to article after article to try and represent what she wanted, but in vain. At last she laid one end of her cloak on the counter and ironed it with her hand. The Greek clapped his hands, while his eyes sparkled, and away he rushed into some back region and brought out the oldest, rustiest affair in the shape of an iron ever beheld—a treasure to us, however; he asked thirty-four piastres (9s.), and took eighteen piastres (3s.), of course a great deal too much for it.

Then we discovered an old tin-man; he was a Turk by the bye (and he lived in a barrel), and he made vessels in tin, which articles it was advisable after buying not to place too near the fire, as their construction was not very strong. The old Turk made treasures for us in the shape of tin pots or jugs, which would hold about a pint; in these we could heat hot water.

The Protestant afternoon service on Sunday (there were no morning prayers) was in one of the wards of the naval hospital. We suppose no other place could have been found; but it was a trial to go there—the smell and atmosphere were both so unhealthy. This condition of the atmosphere of these hospitals arose from the number of cases of frost-bites then under treatment. The arrangements for ventilation were good, and every possible care and attention was shown to the patients.

The Catholic services were performed in a ward of the French naval hospital, the atmosphere of which was even worse than the

British. Every morning the long train of the fifteen Sisters of Mercy was seen slowly wending their way thither; they never, except for this purpose, went beyond the grounds of the embassy.

Our services as nurses were offered to the authorities at the British naval hospital, but were declined, in consequence of their then expecting a party of their own, sent out, of course, by the Admiralty. In the mean time the surgeons said that if any of the nurses could wash for their hospital they would be very thankful, as their washing was three months in arrear. It is a matter of great difficulty to get washing done in Turkey. The surgeons had hired two Maltese women to wash, but both soon ran away.

Miss Stanley appointed some nurses for this work, and a volunteer wished to join; she said as she could not nurse soldiers she would wash for sailors, and for about a month from morning to night she fulfilled her task, which was not a light one. There would be few ladies whose health would have enabled them to undertake such a labour. Two or three of the ladies daily visited the naval hospital to talk to the men, and write letters for them.

They also sent large baskets full of the patients' linen to our house to be mended, and in the evenings we sat round the table in the hall at our work, while one of the party read aloud. Sometimes such a treasure as an English newspaper fell into our hands. It was astonishing how precious a scrap of home news became. We were quite sorry when the mending was done, but with so many hands it did not take long.

Our spirits were beginning to rise at the prospect of work, for negotiations were opened for nurses to be sent to Balaclava; and we heard it was intended to remove the Russian prisoners from the barracks at Koulali, and occupy that building as a British hospital. There was a good deal of sickness among us, not of a serious character, but climatising. The naval surgeons attended those who were ill, and never can they forget the friendly kindness and attention which they received from these gentlemen. In them we indeed found friends in a foreign land.

The weather continued very variable; sometimes the cold was intense; snow would lie on the ground for several days. We suffered much from cold, not that it was so intense as some of the severe frosts in England, but the want of means to warm oneself added so greatly to it. In our large house were two stoves only, which gave but little heat. In the house occupied by the Sisters of Mercy there were no stoves, nothing but charcoal brasiers. It should be remembered that these houses are built solely for summer residences, and are never inhabited in the winter. Blankets we did not possess, so railway wrappers and cloaks were useful beyond expression. One stove was supposed to warm the long hall, which it certainly did not do.

One night some one sitting beside the stove in the hall saw smoke issuing from under the stove plate; she gave the alarm, and we discovered that the plate was laid upon the floor, the woodhouse being underneath. In half-an-hour more the whole would have been in flames, and we turned out on a bitter cold winter evening. As all the houses were built of wood, and there were no engines, the destruction would have been great. Fortunately we were in time to stop it, the only bad consequence being that we were forbidden to have any fire in it at all till the plate was raised on stones from the flooring. This simple operation taking a long time in Turkey, we were for several days in the coldest weather without any fire save a charcoal brasier.

Sometimes after a severe frost would come

a day of spring more bright and lovely than any in England. One Sunday was like this; we watched the fishing from the window. A number of caiques all darted to one particular spot just before our windows, where a shoal of fishes happened to be at little distances; a caique or two were scattered here and there, but the group in the midst was the most remarkable: they struggled and fought who should throw in their nets. It seemed as if they would overturn the caiques. At last in went net after net, and up they came brimful of ilttle silver fishes, and they emptied their nets into the bottom of the boat, and plunged them in again. The heap of fishes glistening in the sunshine, the bright blue Bosphorus smooth as a lake, the dark hills in the distance, the curiously shaped boats and the picturesque dress of the boatmen, their shrill voices, rapid actions, and foreign language, made a picture not easily forgotten, and brought to mind the celebrated cartoon of the miraculous draught. We pleased ourselves with comparing the scene before us to that of the blue lake of Galilee, the eastern hills and Hebrew fishermen.

Immediately behind the Barrack Hospital, quite at the foot of the hills, almost secluded from sight, is the British naval burying ground. It looked a dreary spot then; the grass had not grown over the graves, the rain had made the clay mould wet and muddy. No stone marked who rested there—no sign that they whose remains slept there lay down in a better hope than the poor Turks who were buried close by; no sign that the sleepers were enshrined in the hearts of their country and died in her service.

About halfway up the hill was the French naval burying ground, almost every grave marked by its little wooden cross, with the name of him who was buried there, the ship he belonged to, and the date of his death written on it. True, the wood would in time sink into the earth, but it was pleasing to see the care and thought bestowed. We did not like the contrast between the countries, and the ladies of our party determined to raise a monument to the memories of the sailors and marines who were buried in our burial ground. We had to ask permission for this from the Admiralty, and therefore we could not see our wish carried out before we left Therapia. It was our unanimous wish that it should be a cross to distinguish the burial ground as a Christian one. It now stands in Therapia's British naval burying ground. We afterwards heard that it was badly constructed, and badly placed by the sculptor; nevertheless we trusted the friends of those whose bodies rest beneath that foreign sod would not despise our offering. The stone is inscribed with these words:—

"This stone is raised to the memory of the sailors and marines buried in this graveyard [their names are then inscribed in order] by their countrywomen." On the arms of the cross are engraven the words: " I am the Resurrection and the Life."

Miss Stanley was frequently absent from us for a day or two at a time; her anxiety to have us released from our very unpleasant position was very great. She went frequently to the British embassy at Pera, and met there with much kindness from Lady Stratford, who interested herself warmly in procuring employment for our band. Miss Stanley also went often to Scutari, to try and make arrangements for the reception of some more of her nurses.

During Miss Stanley's absences our anxiety to know our fate grew very intense, and we used to watch for the steamer by which we expected her return eagerly. Two steamers went daily from Buyukdere to Pera, touching at Therapia; one returned at four in the afternoon, the other half-an-hour later. When it touched the quay, loaded with passengers, we looked anxiously for Miss Stanley, or Nicola, the interpreter, who would perhaps bring us letters if she were not there. If she were there she was instantly surrounded by the number of expectant ladies. "Oh, Miss Stanley, what news? Are we going away? Are we to be sent home? What can it all mean?"

Miss Stanley's unvarying answer was that we must be patient, that obstacles were in our way which must be removed ere we could gain admittance to the hospital; she would never say in what these obstacles consisted, and very patiently withstood all our questioning. She was deservedly much beloved by all for her just government of the community, her uniform sweetness of temper and thoughtful kindness for all—but many and bitter were the complaints made of her "vagueness." We could not find out from her why we were detained, and whose fault it was, and that vexed us sadly.

Great excitement also was roused amongst us when the summons came for one or two of the party to leave us for Scutari. This happened twice. Two nurses who were known as very good surgical nurses were sent for. One of these women happened to be a soldier's wife; her chief motive for coming out was to be near her husband. Her friends at home tried to dissuade her from coming, pointing out how very unlikely it was that she should be able to meet with him. She persisted in her wish, and curiously enough the day we entered the Golden Horn he among other sick came down from the camp to Scutari. She did not know this for a week after, and was then prevented by her own illness from going to him for another week. She went at length, and found him dying. She waited on him the last two days of his life, and then after his death remained as nurse for some months.

Next, one of the ladies of our party was

sent for, Miss Nightingale wishing her to take the office of superintendent of the nurses in the General Hospital, Scutari. Great was our anxiety to know what became of our companions. As soon as they left us we heard no more of them; they wrote short notes, saying nothing of what we most wanted to know, viz., their work.

Next came a great move; two ladies, five nuns, and several paid nurses were sent for. We were told at the time that this band composed the whole of those who would be admitted into Scutari Hospital, the rest of the party were to be divided between Balaclava and Koulali, and we waited with as much patience as we could for the conclusion of the arrangements which would open these new fields of labour to us.

Miss Stanley was requested to take the office of superintendent of nurses at Koulali; and she consented to delay her return home for a time and to start the nursing there.

About Balaclava there were many and various opinions; many thought that the Crimea was not sufficiently in the hands of the allies to make it safe for women to go there, that in the event of an attack they would only be a burden, while the hardships they would have to endure would be too great. We were told that, though Miss Nightingale did not forbid it, she would not sanction it. The point was, I believe, decided by Lord Raglan's expressed wish for the assistance of eight nurses.

Miss Nightingale appointed, as superintendent of the Balaclava nursing staff, one of Miss Sellon's sisters under her charge; her seven companions were to be selected from those of our party who should volunteer to go; there were nine volunteers, seven were selected by Miss Stanley, two ladies, five nurses. Great preparations were made for their departure; *rumour* (our only source of information) said that they would find nothing but unfurnished huts at Balaclava; and so the village was ransacked for cooking utensils, as far as the miserable shops of Therapia would furnish; bedsteads and bedding were packed, and all was ready.

A note from Miss Stanley (who was staying at the embassy in Pera) announced that passages were taken on board the "Melbourne" for the party for Balaclava; that the superintendent would go on board in the Golden Horn; that the "Melbourne" would lie off Therapia sufficient time to allow the party to go on board, but that all the luggage must be embarked in caiques, and those lie off the house ready to start as soon as the "Melbourne" should lay to. She was to sail on the 15th of January; early on that day the caique with well-loaded luggage lay off the quay before the house.

The party were all ready dressed, and every eye watched the vessels as they passed; but the day wore on, and no ship lay to off

Therapia. When night came on a general sense of disappointment fell on all the Balaclava party. We had grown so familiar with suspense and disappointment that they were not satisfied with our assurances that ships hardly ever sailed on the day they professed to do; they could not be persuaded but that some obstacle had arisen. When the next morning came, six of the party declared they could not bear to spend the day as they had done the preceding one, with their bonnets on, watching the ships; they would employ themselves in some way, and be ready at five minutes' notice. One lady of the party, the one who had washed at the hospital, and who was especially distinguished for her self-devotion, had been from the first most anxious to go to Balaclava; she was sorely afraid some obstacle had arisen from this delay in the "Melbourne," and she would not wait like the others, but dressed ready as before.

The day was stormy, the Bosphorus very rough. Nicola came directly after breakfast to say that the caidjee declared it was too rough for him to lie off the quay; he must go into a little bay opposite the village. Our friend would not lose sight of her boxes, so she insisted upon going thither with him, and seated herself among the boxes in the caique, and patiently kept her place the whole morning. As little groups of our party passed down the quay for walking or shopping, there they found her settled. How we laughed! She did not care a bit, but took it all in good part. To crown the whole, early in the afternoon a vessel was seen in the distance; it would have taken nearly an hour to ascertain whether it was the "Melbourne" —we could not even see her colours; but our friend could not wait, so off the caique and boxes and lady went, over the billows of the Bosphorus, which were many and fierce that day, till it lay alongside the vessel. The lady boarded her and found she was French, the captain very polite, but could give her no information respecting the "Melbourne." Again the lady seated herself in her caique; we watching from our windows saw the little dark speck dancing on the waves. "Surely she is coming home now," we said. "She certainly will be drowned on this rough day;" and, exclaimed one of the Balaclava party, "She has got all our boxes with her, and *they* will all be lost!"

Another sail was seen on the horizon, and we saw the little speck turn in that direction, and soon lie alongside this vessel. Though we were really alarmed at the freak, it was impossible to help laughing at the pertinacity with which she pursued her object. At this juncture one of the naval surgeons came in and joined in the laugh, but soon said, "Really it is too rough for such an adventure. I hope she has two caidjee with her." "No, indeed; only one," we answered. He instantly ran out and ordered a caique with two rowers to follow our adventurous friend. However, before it could reach her she had returned in safety, and her mind at rest. The second vessel was English, and the officer in charge knew the "Melbourne" was still in dock, and had not finished coaling. So now all were satisfied, and it was well, for three more days of suspense were their portion. At length, on the 19th at noon, the "Melbourne" lay off Therapia, and the party were soon safely on board.

## CHAPTER IV.

The Establishment at Therapia broken up—Scutari Barrack Hospital—Domestic arrangements—The kitchen—The Ladies' quarters—A sad evening walk—Distribution of the work—Moments of despondency—The diet roll—Serious objections to some of the regulations respecting it—Inefficient state of the purveying department—Miss Nightingale's die$^t$ kitchen—The orderly and the indignant nurse—The Inspector-General's order respecting cooking in the wards—Military discipline out of season—The general hospital, Scutari—The British burying ground—The cemetery of the Turks—An unkind orderly—The Valley of the Shadow of Death—Clean linen—Comparative uselessness of the free gift store—Prevalence of sickness amongst the nurses—Details of their daily life—Untempered misery—More guests—Those who died and those whom they left behind them—How the story will be told—Letters home.

THE day at last arrived when the establishment at Therapia was finally broken up.

Seven had gone to Balaclava; three hired nurses had been sent home (one from ill-health, two from their habits of intoxication); two more hired nurses had been sent to private cases at Pera, while waiting for Government work (they afterwards joined the Koulali nursing staff); eighteen were received at Scutari, and the remaining sixteen under Miss Stanley's charge, went to Koulali. We will now follow the footsteps of those proceeding to Scutari. We landed at the wharf, and climbing the steep hill found ourselves at the main guard or principal entrance to Scutari barrack hospital. The hospital is an immense square building; three long corridors run completely round it, and it is three stories high. Numberless apartments open out of all these corridors, which are called wards. At each corner of the building is a tower. The main guard divides A corridor; turning to the left after passing through one or two divisions from which the guard rooms open, we came to the sick.

To avoid the cold air of the long corridor, wooden partitions were put up, and the spaces between these were called divisions. We made our way through the double row of sick to the tower at the corner (Miss Nightingale's quarters); the smell in this corridor of sick was quite overpowering—they were almost all surgical cases, which, I suppose, was partly the cause.

On arriving at Miss Nightingale's quarters we entered the large kitchen or hall, from which all the other rooms opened. There were four rooms on the lower story occupied as follows:—Mr. and Mrs. Bracebridge in one; Miss Nightingale in another; the five nuns in the third; fourteen nurses and one lady in the last. A staircase led up the tower to two other rooms; the first occupied by the sisters from Miss Sellon's and other ladies; the second by the nurses belonging to St. John's Training Institution. The kitchen was used as Miss Nightingale's extra-diet kitchen. From this room were distributed quantities of arrowroot, sago, rice puddings, jelly, beef-tea, and lemonade, upon requisitions made by the surgeons. This caused great comings to and fro; numbers of orderlies were waiting at the door with requisitions. One of the nuns or a lady received them, and saw they were signed and countersigned, and then served them.

We used, among ourselves, to call this kitchen the tower of Babel, from the variety of languages spoken in it and the confusion. In fact, in the middle of the day everything and everybody seemed to be there. Boxes, parcels, bundles of sheets, shirts, and old linen and flannels; tubs of butter, sugar, bread, kettles, saucepans, heaps of books, and of all kinds of rubbish, besides the "diets," which were being dispensed; then the people, ladies, nuns, nurses, orderlies, Turks, Greeks, French and Italian servants, officers, and others waiting to see Miss Nightingale; all passing to and fro, all intent upon their own business, and all speaking their own language.

The ladies' quarters were the first room upstairs. It was a good-sized one, with eight windows, and having a fine view of the sea. A divan ran round the room, covered with stuffed cushions, which, together with the matting, were well furnished with fleas. A number of rats also lived in the divan and wainscoting, and took nightly promenades about the room.

On Tuesday mornings a Turk came to hoist the Turkish flag from the summit of the tower. He therefore passed through our room at sunrise to put it up, and at sunset to take it down: he always omitted the ceremony of knocking at the door, and as he always took off his shoes also, it was not very easy to discern his approach.

Two days after my arrival, Miss Nightingale sent for me to go with her round the hospital. (Miss Nightingale generally visited her special cases at night). We went round the whole of the second story, into many of the wards and into one of the upper corridors. It seemed an endless walk, and it was one not easily forgotten. As we slowly passed along, the silence was profound; very seldom did a moan or cry from those multitudes of deeply suffering ones fall on our ears. A dim light burnt here and there. Miss Nightingale carried her lantern, which she would set down before she bent over any of the patients. I much admired Miss Nightingale's manner to the men—it was so tender and kind.

All the corridors were thickly lined with beds laid on low tressels raised a few inches from the ground. In the wards a divan runs round the room, and on this were laid the straw beds, and the sufferers on them. The hospital was crowded to its fullest extent. The building, which has since been reckoned to hold, with comfort, seventeen hundred men, then held between three and four thousand. Miss Nightingale assigned me my work—it was half A corridor, the whole of B, half C, the whole of I, (on the third story), and all the wards leading out of these respective corridors; in each corridor there were fifteen of these, except in No. 1, where there were only six. This work I was to share with another lady and one nurse. The number of patients under our charge was, as far as I could reckon, about fifteen hundred.

Miss Nightingale told us only to attend to those in the divisions of those surgeons who wished for our services. She said the staff-surgeon of the division was willing we should work under him, and she charged us never to do anything for the patients without the leave of the doctors.

When we had gone round the hospital we came out of A corridor upon the main guard

The blast of cold air from the entrance was refreshing after the overpowering smell of the wards. The corridors of the lower story were under the charge of Miss E——, from Miss Sellon's, assisted by nurses; the remainder of A, under Sister M. S——, of the Bermondsey nuns; the upper corridors, except No. I., under another nun. Several nurses were engaged in different divisions of C corridor; the rest in the diet kitchen.

It seems simply impossible to describe Scutari Hospital at this time. Far abler pens have tried, and all, in some measure, failed; for what an eye-witness saw was past description. Even those who read the harrowing accounts in the "Times" and elsewhere, could not have imagined the full horror of the reality. As we passed the corridors, we asked ourselves if it was not a terrible dream. When we woke in the morning, our hearts sank down at the thought of the woe we must witness that day. At night we lay down wearied beyond expression; but not so much from physical fatigue, though that was great, as from the sickness of heart from living amidst that mass of hopeless suffering. On all sides prevailed the utmost confusion—whose fault it was I cannot tell—clear heads have tried to discover in vain: probably the blame should have been shared by all the departments of the hospital.

It is necessary here to particularise some of the hospital rules to give an idea of our work. First, the diet roll. In London hospitals a diet card for each patient hangs at the head of his bed, and any alteration in it is generally, if not always, made by the house-surgeon. In military hospitals the diet roll is a book of foolscap paper, with a sheet for each day, and small divisions for each diet. Whatever is inserted in the diet rolls (as in all hospitals), cannot be furnished till the next day. In military hospitals a man is placed either on full, half, low, or spoon diet. If a man is on full diet, one column is sufficient, as by it is understood that he is to have daily 1lb. of meat, ditto of bread, ditto of potatoes, and two pints of tea, also half-a-pint of porter. Half-diet is exactly the half of this. Low-diet the half again of that. Spoon-diet is simply one pound of bread and two pints of tea; but it has this difference, that the surgeon may give a man on spoon-diet extras; but for any patient on full, half, or low diet he may not: nor may the surgeons order more than two or three extras to the spoon-diets—the extras at this time were fowls, mutton chops, potatoes, milk, eggs, arrowroot, rice, sago, and lemons for lemonade.

Before the diet roll could be sent into the purveyor's stores it had to be signed by the assistant-surgeon in charge of the patients, whose names were inserted on it, and then it had to be countersigned by the staff-surgeon of the division. The staff-surgeon being the assistant-surgeon's superior officer, and medical etiquette entirely sinking in military discipline, it is quite possible that an assistant-surgeon may be called to account for any extravagance in the diet roll, and this sometimes happened, for extravagance seemed to be the great bugbear of our Eastern hospitals.

The diet rolls were written by the sergeants or corporals appointed as ward masters; if they made any mistake (which they very often did) there was no redress. If they had forgotten to insert an extra to such a name, he must for that day go without it.

The purveying department was at that time in a most inefficient state; constantly the requirements of the diet rolls were not complied with, the stores were given out most irregularly, the orderlies were often obliged to go down to the store-rooms at four A.M. to draw the rations for breakfast;

the last of the band would not be served till past seven A.M. The men's dinners, which ought to have come at twelve, often did not come till five or six P.M.—three P.M. was thought excellent time. Very often we saw the orderlies cutting up the carcases of sheep in the corridor close by the beds in which were men suffering from every form of disease.

Of course many cases must arise in which the patients are in such a state that their diet must be altered or added to that day. The means of doing this is by a requisition signed by the assistant-surgeon. He must write a separate requisition for each man, and after he has signed it, it is taken to the staff-surgeon to be countersigned, and then to the stores.

This regulation, and indeed all others, were made for military hospitals in an ordinary state, when the buildings only hold the numbers they are intended for, where every department is sufficiently supplied with people to work it, where extreme cases are to be counted in each ward by ones and twos, and can then of course receive the full attention of the surgeon; but these same laws brought to bear in the Eastern hospitals in that unprecedented time of distress became useless—extreme cases in Scutari were counted by one or two hundreds—it was a matter of impossibility for surgeons to write requisitions enough for their patients' wants, especially as they had to be countersigned by the staff-surgeon, a man having a large charge besides many other duties, and who was never sure of being found in any one place after the regular hours of going his rounds. The purveying department was also so utterly inefficient that constantly requisitions were signed and sent in, and then not honoured.

Miss Nightingale's diet kitchen has been before mentioned; the articles supplied from thence were intended for spoon diets only, and could only be obtained by a requisition signed and countersigned; a great number of requisitions were sent in to Miss Nightingale's extra diet kitchen, but very far short of the number required. That this was so will appear from the following fact,—the surgeons would constantly give us *verbal* permission to give a man nourishment or stimulants. We never for an instant thought of giving anything without this permission (I mean the ladies and Sisters of Mercy, not the hired nurses, who in this as in many other matters often could not be trusted).

We well knew that a man may apparently be sinking for want of food or stimulants, while his medical attendant would know it was the very worst thing for him; but when we received this verbal permission we had no means of getting anything for the patients. We used to receive such orders as these: "No. 1, give him anything you like. No. 2, he may have anything he can fancy. No. 3, keep him up as much as possible ;" and so on. Drinks for the fever patients were allowed in quantities could we only have had the materials to make them with. We could not get the assistant-surgeons to write out the number of requisitions which were necessary in order to procure these materials. At last some of us persuaded one or two of our surgeons to write a requisition for dry stores; that is, for tins of preserved beef-tea, and for lemons and sugar to make lemonade. This was at first most successful. Many of the assistant-surgeons gladly accepted anything we prepared for the men. One difficulty only remained, *i. e.* hot water. It was of course necessary to make the beef-tea, and also for the lemonade, as the water was so unwholesome it could not be used without boiling. We contrived to boil water in small quantities on the stoves in the corridors and wards. It was a slow process, but still we succeeded.

The orderlies seemed roused from the state of apathy into which the distress around and the apparent impossibility of getting anything for the patients had thrown them, and they assisted us in every possible way. Some of the orderlies looked with eager eyes on us as we carried round the small quantities of beef tea, for it was of course only to the patients belonging to the surgeons who wrote the requisitions that we could give the articles. One night a lady and her nurse were going round with some beef tea, when an orderly came up, and in a tone of entreaty pointed to a poor man. He was very bad, said he, "and some of that stuff would do him good, and the doctor said he might have anything he could fancy." The nurse turned round quick upon him.

"Orderly!"

"Yes, nurse!"

"What's the use of your asking unpossibilities? You know very well that we can't give this beef-tea to your men. You must get your doctor to write a requisition for a tin of beef-tea!"

"Oh, very well, nurse," said the orderly, "I will."

"But that is not all," replied she; "at the same time get him to write a requisition for hot water!"

Our plan of thus helping the men was put a stop to by an order from Dr. Cumming, the inspector-general, that no cooking was to be done in the wards, and thus our only means of assisting the men was ended.

We seldom dressed the wounds, as there were dressers who performed this office, and the greater number of our patients were cases of fever and dysentery, who needed constant attention and nourishment, frequently administered in small quantities, and this we were now not suffered to give. All the diets not issued from Miss Nightingale's kitchen were of such a bad quality, and so wretchedly cooked, that the men often could not eat them. After a man had been put on half or even full diet, the surgeons were often obliged to return him to spoon diet from his not being able to eat the meat.

It was very hard work after Dr. Cumming's order had been issued to pace the corridor and hear perhaps the low voice of a fever patient, "Give me a drink for the love of God," and have none to give—for water we dared not give to any; or to see the look of disappointment on the faces of those to whom we had been accustomed to give the beef tea. The assistant-surgeons were very sorry, they said, for the alteration, but they had no power to help it—their duty was only to obey. On one occasion an assistant-surgeon told us that Dr. Cumming had threatened to arrest him for having allowed a man too many extras on the diet roll. Amid all the confusion and distress of Scutari hospital, military discipline was never lost sight of, and an infringement of one of its smallest observances was worse than letting twenty men die from neglect.

The General Hospital, Scutari, stands about a mile from the Barrack Hospital; it is built close to the cliff, and commands a most beautiful view of Constantinople and the Sea of Marmora. It is a very fine building, not so large as the Barrack, and it holds with ease one thousand men, allowing room for doctors, chaplains, nurses, &c. The nurses at the General Hospital were then superintended by Miss Smythe, who shortly afterwards went to Koulali, and assisting her were three of Miss Sellon's sisters, one lady, five nuns of the community called the "Kinsale Nuns," and I think about ten nurses. The ladies had a diet kitchen, and the routine was the same as at the Barrack Hospital.

When we went out for a walk it was generally to this hospital, or to the cliff around it. On one side of the General Hospital is the British burying ground, a spot which we could never visit without emotion, for there rested, oh! how many of England's noble sons! Whenever we went they were digging graves, for from fifty to seventy a day were interred. Once we saw the cart loaded with the bodies coming slowly along, but we turned away, for the sight was too much to bear. The burying ground is beautifully situated, just on the edge of the cliff—the sea lies spread before it. On one side in the distance lies Constantinople; on the opposite shore, far beyond where the eye can reach, stretches the great cemetery of the Turks, thickly studded with cypresses, and the strange tombstones of various colours, with their different devices, the turban, the broken lily, and other heathen emblems. Dark and gloomy looks the vast cemetery whither the Turk prays to be borne, that, when European Turkey shall become the property of the Christian, his bones may rest with his fathers.

Brightly in the open sunshine under no dark cypress' shade rest Britain's loved and lost. Here and there a stone or wooden cross marks in Whose name and in what hope we laid them down. The blue waves sparkle beneath their resting-place; the birds sing sweetly over their graves; the grass grows green over the mound, and in their countrypeople's hearts the spot must ever be sacred.

Returning from our walk over the wide plain which lies between the two hospitals, one's heart was weighed down by the thought of that mighty mass of suffering inside those walls, the sounds of which, though unheard by men, went up to the ear of Heaven. The thought of its immensity and apparent hopelessness was oppressive beyond description. All that was done for relief seemed but a drop in the ocean, and ere things could get to rights, or order be restored, how many hundreds of precious lives would have passed away!

Day succeeded day with little variation, and suffering and agony went on and on, and the angel of death stayed not his hand, but went swiftly day and night through those corridors and wards and took hundreds with him as he passed. In the morning when we entered our wards sad it was to see the numbers of empty beds.

In B corridor at one time were two cases of fever in a very bad state. The orderly attending them was a brute; he never did anything for them unless desired by the surgeon or nurse, and all the poor creatures did in the wildness of their delirium he treated as if it was done on purpose. He declared that they *would* tear the wet rags from their heads, and it was no use to put them on again, and he never replaced them unless we obliged him; he used to put down their food by their sides, just as if they were strong and sensible, and able to help themselves, instead of the poor hands lying helpless by their sides, or clutching and picking the bed clothes, the unerring sign to those who know sickness well that their days on earth were numbered.

Poor fellows! their passage through the valley of the shadow of death was hard indeed. They lingered many days. Among so very many others we could not give them much time. One day passing by their beds I saw one of them was near death. I was obliged to go to our quarters on an errand for another patient. I made all possible haste, and in a quarter of an hour returned to the bed of death, but the bed was vacant—he had died, been wrapped in his blanket, and carried away to the dead house—the other died that night.

Death indeed became familiar to us as the ordinary events of life. Among one thousand five hundred sick committed to the care of three women, it was impossible to attend to the greater number, and it was grievous to be obliged to pass by so many sick on whom we longed to wait—cases like some of spotted fever in A corridor—and see the poor hands grasping the sheets, and the sufferer in his delirium refusing the medicine on which his life hung.

The want of clean linen was bitterly felt at that time in Scutari. How it was issued from the stores was a mystery no one could ever unravel. If things were sent to be washed they never returned, and there was not the slightest order or regularity in the issue of linen, either sheets or shirts. Towels and pocket-handkerchiefs were both considered unnecessary luxuries for the soldiers, and could be obtained only from Miss Nightingale's free-gift store, and, generally speaking, only from them could flannel shirts be had. Orderlies thought nothing of taking off a soiled flannel from a man and giving him a clean cotton in exchange.

Confusion, indeed, so prevailed in all quarters at that unhappy time, that though quantities of things were sent to Scutari but few ever reached the sufferers for whom they were destined. Every ship that came in brought to Miss Nightingale large packages of every imaginable article of wearing apparel; great numbers of bales of old linen and lint also arrived, and these last were quite useless, as both were amply supplied from the medical stores of the hospital.

The packages were unpacked and put into Miss Nightingale's free-gift store, which was a large shed outside the hospital. It was impossible for Miss Nightingale, with her numerous and arduous avocations, to find time even to look at them; no one had the regular charge of them; nurses and sometimes ladies when they had time went to assist at the endless task of putting them to rights. There was another store inside the hospital, which was under the charge of the Superioress of the Sisters of Mercy; this store was kept in beautiful order, but was quite full. From neither of these stores of Miss Nightingale could anything be procured but on the same plan as the diets, *i. e.*, a doctor's requisition signed and countersigned. It was even more impossible to get these than the others for diets, from a feeling amongst the surgeons that clothing for the men ought to have come from Government stores, and not liking fully to acknowledge the gross neglect of the purveying department. So we only saw how miserably the men were off, and were obliged to leave them so.

It was a common thing to find men with sheets and shirts unchanged for weeks. I have opened the collar of a patient's shirt and found it literally lined with vermin. It was common to find men covered with sores from lying in one position on the hard straw beds and coarse sheets, and there were no pillows to put under them. Pillows were unknown to the Government stores, and we could not get requisitions for them from Miss Nightingale's free gift store. The only exceptions to this rule were that some articles which were given to the nurses they gave away to the patients. Mrs. Bracebridge gave away numbers of things from the free gift store, chiefly to those who assisted in the unpacking of them. By this means we sometimes gained possession of shirts, or pocket handkerchiefs, or towels, and they were much prized by the men.

A great deal of sickness prevailed among ourselves; two nurses at this time were lying ill with fever, one not expected to live; two out of the five nuns were in the same state—they both lay for days at the point of death, but ultimately recovered. During the whole of their illness they remained in the room where the three other sisters slept and ate. There was no infirmary to remove the sick ladies to. The sick nurses were taken to a room outside the hospital. Of those among ladies and nurses not ill with fever many were laid up for a day or two at a time from over fatigue and want of proper food.

Our life was a laborious one; we had to sweep our own room, make our beds, wash up our dishes, &c., and fetch our meals from the kitchen below. We went to our wards at nine, returned at two, went again at three (unless we went out for a walk, which we had permission to do at this hour), returned at half-past five to tea, then to the wards again till half-past nine, and often again for an hour to our special cases. We had prayers read by Mr. Bracebridge at eight in the morning, and at nine at night one of the chaplains came; but at that time they were often prevented from press of work. We suffered greatly from want of proper food. Our diet consisted of the coarse sour bread of the country, tea without milk, butter so rancid we could not touch it, and very bad meat and porter; and at night a glass of wine or brandy. It was an effort even to those in health to sit down to our meals; we forced the food down as a duty, but some of the ladies became so weak and ill they really could not touch it. For one in particular we tried to get a little milk or an egg, but both these articles were scarce; a small quantity of both was taken into Miss Nightingale's and Mr. and Mrs. Bracebridge's rooms, but could not be furnished to the rest of the party. Occasionally Miss Nightingale kindly sent some light dish from her own table to the sick ladies. The nuns took all their meals in their own apartments, the nurses in theirs, the ladies in theirs: Miss Nightingale and Mr. and Mrs. Bracebridge in their own apartment.

The quantity of vermin in the wards was

Often did our hearts burn within us as we passed along, as we heard the thanks and blessings poured upon those who were doing oh! so miserably little for so great affliction; or as we knelt by the dying to hear his last request to write home and tell them all about him; or as we watched the death struggle, and saw one noble heart after another cease to beat.

The sick came in almost daily, so that the beds which death had emptied during the night were sure to be filled again in the course of the day. Sad it was to see the sick coming in, the orderlies putting down the stretchers and looking round in despair for a bed to lay the poor sufferer on: a low moan was the only evidence of the torture he was enduring, or how he longed to be laid in any place where he could die in peace. Then again they hastily raised the stretcher on their shoulder, giving frequent jerks to the agonised frame, and turned down another corridor in search of a bed. "Patience, deeply-suffering ones," we whispered to ourselves, "all is not forgotten, every drop in this most bitter cup is portioned out for you, and as you drink it will be treasured up in heaven. You have followed bravely an earthly captain to victory through wounds and over dying comrades, follow now the Great Captain of your salvation through the dark valley."

Sickness is sad at all times—sad is it to languish and suffer on our soft English beds, with skilful physicians full of anxiety, with tender nurses and loving friends, with every comfort earth can give; but only those who saw can enter into the dreariness of those sick beds. It was so sad to see them die one after another—we learned to love them so—ever ringing in our ears seemed the anxious hopes and prayers of the fond hearts in England. The mother's only stay was there, or the loved husband or brother, and they were dying, not in the glory of the battle field, but in these dreary corridors. They who had fought so bravely suffered so nobly; they who, if they had lived, would have been honoured by a nation's gratitude—they were passing away by hundreds—no name would mark their graves, and they would, save in the loving hearts of home, be soon forgotten.

No, not forgotten either. Surely when the tale of that memorable winter shall be told, when future generations shall hear how they stormed at Alma, charged at Balaclava, and held their ground at Inkermann; how they resolutely waited before the walls of Sebastopol, till at length the gallantly defended city yielded to her dauntless foes—England will not forget those who shed their blood for her sake, though no glory hovered round their death-bed, save a ray from His glory who first taught us to be "obedient unto death." Sad it was to hear the tales they would tell, such mere boys as some of them were, how they had enlisted in a moment of folly and bitterly regretted it, or to listen to their long accounts of friends at home; how they would describe every little incident relating to them as if it were engraven on their hearts.

Very often we wrote letters home for them from their dictation; we sat on their beds to do it, for there were no other seats of any kind. It often struck us the eagerness with which they accepted our offer to write a letter for any of them—they hardly ever asked us to do so—they seemed to be so resigned to everything, that it was quite a surprise to them to be able to have a sheet of paper and an envelope placed at their disposal, still more a friend's hand to write for them; and then they were so full of solicitude—"Were we not too tired to do it? or was it not uncomfortable sitting on that there bed?"

## CHAPTER V.

Koulali—Roads in Turkey—Koulali Barrack Hospital—Peculiar construction of the wards—The Convalescent Hospital—Character of the scenery about Koulali—The General Hospital—The sick from the trenches—Classification of wards—Hospital diet arrangements—Sickness amongst the nurses.

AFTER a fortnight had been spent among these scenes, a change occurred in the nursing arrangements. Miss Stanley at Koulali was in great want of additional hands, as she found her staff inefficient to the work of the hospitals of Koulali, and requested help from Miss Nightingale. Miss N. gave leave to all the ladies at Scutari to volunteer for Koulali. Miss Smythe and myself did so, and another lady followed us in a few days.

Koulali is about five miles north of Scutari. I once went there from Scutari in a Turkish carriage; the drive was for some distance through the Turkish cemetery, which, as I said before, extends for miles round Scutari. There are no roads in Turkey worthy of the name, nor have the carriages any springs; between these two misfortunes one runs a chance of being jolted to death. Certainly I never expected to reach Koulali with whole bones, and firmly determined as it was my first drive in a Turkish carriage it should be my last.

Koulali barracks are built on the banks of the Bosphorus, a few yards from the quay; the depth of water allows steamers to come alongside the quay, therefore its facility for landing the sick is very great. The hospital is a square red building three stories high in front, very much smaller than Scutari, but a large building nevertheless. The principal entrance is raised a few feet from the quay, ascending which you pass under the archway into the barrack-yard. Apartments are built over the archway, called the Sultan's apartments, at that time occupied by the commandant, chaplains, and medical officers. Standing under the archway, to the right and left, were the wards, which extended more than halfway round the square, two stories high. Opposite were stables, which were then about to be made into wards.

The wards were of a very peculiar construction, a long corridor, with a gallery over it; the doors of almost all open upon the different entrances of the hospital, which all have archways. This made the wards seem like separate buildings, though on the upper story, by passing through rooms, one can walk from one end of the hospital to the other, only descending at the different entrances. The three entrances were all guarded by sentries. Built in continuation of the hospital on the quay are more rooms and stables, occupied by the Turkish soldiers; beyond this comes the riding-school, which was just then converted into the convalescent hospital: a most delightful one it made. It was divided into twelve wards, partitioned off by wood-work about eleven feet high; the roof was high with open beams. This hospital was well warmed and ventilated; there was an apartment for the surgeon in charge— and the surgery and kitchen were built off.

The situation was delightful, as all those able to walk could get outside the hospital and catch the fresh breeze from the sea. Hills rose immediately around Koulali; it was literally shut in on all sides between hills and water. Great fears were entertained at that time that in the heat of summer this would render it unhealthy; these fears were, however, happily never realised. On the first hill above the Barrack Hospital, on the Scutari side, was built the General Hospital. The Turks always appear to build an hospital close to their barracks. Both buildings were now British hospitals. We distinguished them as Barrack and General hospitals, or sometimes upper and lower. It was a good climb up the hill to the General Hospital, but one was rewarded by the fresh air and lovely view.

The General Hospital was built on the plan of Scutari—two stories high, corridor running round, and wards out of them. It held with comfort two hundred and fifty men, with apartments for medical officers and nurses. Of course at that time many more were obliged to be accommodated. At the upper hospital apartments were provided for the Catholic Sisters of Mercy, some of whom came down to nurse in wards at the barrack hospitals, while a few ladies and nurses went up to help the rest of the sisters in the General Hospital. Our apartments were in one corner of the lower hospital, for at each corner there was a small corridor, with half-a-dozen small rooms opening out of it. Among these rooms there was a very small kitchen, which, however, we contrived to make our extra diet kitchen. A dark closet formed our store-room. There was one large kitchen for the general use, where the meat for the full and half diets was cooked; but the hospital was so crowded, the cookery arrangements so wretched, that our aid in cooking the spoon diets was gladly accepted by the doctors.

In the hospitals of Koulali at that time were very few wounded. The wounded of Alma and Inkermann had either recovered or died. It was the sick from the trenches who poured down upon us. Fever, dysentery, diarrhœa, and frost-bite were our four principal diseases, and the sufferers were those who, having struggled with disease to the last, came down with their constitutions broken and needing careful nursing. We were received and treated from first to last with the utmost cordiality, courtesy, and kindness by the army surgeons. Dr. Tice was then principal medical officer, succeeded shortly after by Dr. Humphrey. The principal medical officer was of course the one under whose immediate orders we were placed. By these gentlemen we were treated with uniform kindness; they instructed us in what way we could be most useful, and always spoke warmly of the assistance we rendered them.

The wards of Koulali hospital were classified: No. 2, surgical; No. 3, fever; No. 4, dysentery; No. 5, diarrhœa; No. 6, dysentery. Every ward was full. We had then one thousand men, with very few exceptions all confined to bed, and hardly a case not a most serious one. Our duties were to accompany the surgeon round the wards to receive his orders for the day, then attending to the food and medicine, seeing to the linen, and feeding those too weak to feed themselves. (This is one instance where nurses are wanted to carry out the surgeon's orders. He may order a man medicine, wine, and nourishment, and the article be furnished, and then the orderly sets it down by the patient's side and thinks no more about it, whilst the patient is perhaps weaker than an infant, or unconscious of what he is doing.) Then came writing letters, procuring books for those a little better and able to read—newspapers were always precious, but at that time an untold boon.

Our plan was to receive the surgeon's *verbal* orders for the men's food, and if there was any difficulty about the requisitions, or when the requisitions were procured having them honoured by the purveyor, we supplied them out of our own kitchen. The doctors constantly left numbers of cases in our charge to be fed as we thought best. Whenever a verbal order was given, the lady or sister wrote her own requisition on the ladies' diet-kitchen and it was immediately attended to, as far as our Free Gift's Store would allow. In the evenings the surgeons visited their wards; then came the night-drinks' distribution, sorely needed by all, for thirst was acutely felt by the frostbitten and dysentery as well as the fever patients. Late at night, very weary, we sought our quarters. Gladly would we have undertaken night work, but our numbers were far from adequate for the labour of the day. All had a far larger portion than was commensurate to their strength, and only by God's especial help did we keep up at all.

Almost immediately on our arrival two of our party, being ill, were removed to the Hotel des Croissants, Buyukdere, twelve miles down the Bosphorus, on the European side. The next day they sickened with fever. One paid nurse accompanied them. One of the nuns fell ill with fever the following day, so our number was reduced to eighteen for both hospitals.

The same day the Misses ——— left; we

had hardly seen them off in a caique when an alarm that our quarter was on fire burst upon our ears. It proceeded from the kitchen, and it was discovered that the flue of the chimney had been so built that if it got heated it must catch fire. This was a common specimen of Turkish building. In five minutes the engineer officer and his men were on the spot, and by their prompt and vigorous efforts the fire, which was now bursting out, was arrested. Two engines played for five hours before danger was over, and then what a scene! The kitchen unroofed, the wall of one bedroom broken in, and the corridor a floating mass of mud, water, and stones—another room so stuffed with furniture we could not move.

The frost was just beginning to set in. We stood in the barrack-yard watching the devastation with resignation, and wondering where we should sleep that night. We did not wonder long, for the officers and chaplains with ready kindness offered us the choice of their quarters. We accepted the principal room in the Sultan's quarters, which the commandant vacated for our use; two of the bedrooms in the old quarters were sufficiently habitable to accommodate the three nurses.

From this time the whole party of ladies ate, drank, and slept in one apartment. We felt that Miss Stanley who filled so arduous and responsible a position needed a separate room and more tempting food than at that time fell to our lot; but although her health suffered from these causes she resolutely refused to have any luxuries or comforts in which all those about her could not partake.

To add to our troubles, the next day one of the three nurses sickened with fever. Of course each separate case of fever among ourselves not only caused the loss of the invalid from the nursing staff, but the principal, if not the whole, services of another to attend upon her.

## CHAPTER VI.

Establishment of an extra-diet kitchen — Rough luxuries—Dismissal of a nurse and her attempt to commit suicide—Arrival of Irish soldiers at the Hospital—Terrible cases of frost-bites—Private Fitzgerald—News of the death of the Russian Emperor—An earthquake—The Russian prisoners—Distressing cases of delirium—Zeal and admirable conduct of the Sisters of Mercy.

How were we to supply our "extra diet" kitchen, how prepare the food on which so many depended? The erection of a shed in the barrack-yard was immediately set on foot; but it took ten days ere we gained possession of it, and our only resource was three or four small charcoal brasiers. Charcoal always drawing so much more quickly in the open air, we placed them in the barrack-yard.

"Misfortunes never come singly;" so we thought when John, the soldier cook, fell sick and had to go into the fever ward. Then the thaw came, and the yard was a mass of snow and black mud, and then it alternately froze and thawed, making our weary hours in the barrack-yard seem long indeed. Our cook ill, we cooked for ourselves, our only staff being Henry, a sailor lad, and the Greeks, who had not the slightest conscience as to appropriating anything that pleased them; serious indeed was our loss if they did, for our "free gift" store was very scanty, and of course we could only draw the exact quantity allowed by the diet roll, so that an egg once lost was not easily replaced; an ounce of arrowroot or sugar was worth more than its weight in gold, while a saucepan to boil it in, or a spoon to stir it with, was guarded by its fortunate possessors with a dragon-like vigilance.

After ten days we gained possession of a

kitchen, which was in two divisions, one was in the Sultan's quarters, the other the shed in the yard; John recovered and took charge of the first, Henry of the shed; part of the cookery was carried on in one, and the rest in the other. Great joy was caused by a gift of Lady Stratford de Redcliffe of a large stove for charcoal, upon which we could fry as well as boil. Lady Stratford had given the stove some time before but it could not be used till it could be placed in a kitchen.

Our quarters which had been burned were now refitted; and we should have returned thither had not the officers most kindly insisted upon making the exchange, thus relinquishing the best rooms to our use; namely, four rooms in the Sultan's quarters, of which one we used ourselves, one as an infirmary, and two were occupied by the nurses. Dr. and Mrs. Tice and the two Church of England chaplains occupied the remainder of the rooms on the left side of the archway. The Bey who commanded the Turkish troops lived on the right side; and we had a room to keep our stores in instead of a dark closet.

By slow and strenuous efforts we gradually improved the state of the kitchen. We were able by means of our stove to fry a small quantity of chops. In one of the boilers in our kitchen shed we boiled fowls, and then cut them in half for the patients. Another boiler contained water for arrowroot; everything was on the roughest scale; the orderlies brought large cans or wooden buckets, put their arrowroot and cold water into them, and stirred it up with a bit of stick; then Henry dispensed the boiling water, and of course the orderlies fought who should get it first. The lady in charge put in the wine, and the arrowroot was carried to the sister or lady in charge of each ward, and dispensed to the men. Persons accustomed to make the delicate food for some dear invalid, or who have watched the beautiful order of the kitchen of a London hospital, will smile at our extra diets for the sick; nevertheless they were gladly received by the poor sufferers, who thought them an improvement upon *nothing*.

But the labour of life was lemonade. The patients suffered much from thirst, and those who were ordered lemonade were very numerous. The sight of a lemon squeezer (no such article could be furnished from the stores) would have been very gratifying, the cutting and squeezing were so long and tiresome. We employed the Greeks about it, but their help was not to be depended on; sometimes they would work, at others suddenly depart for hours; and they would, moreover, pocket lemons, or other things to any extent. Besides, all the Greeks in Government employ went home at sunset; and the chief call for lemonade was in the evenings. One evening a lady made a large pailful, and went into the "dark closet" for sugar; she put it into the lemonade, stirred it up and tasted it to see if all was right, but it was salt she had put in instead of sugar; and wearily did she set about the task of making more; cut more lemons, and get more water—all the water came from a tank at the extreme end of the barrack yard, and had to be fetched by Greeks, who took an enormous time about it, so that water became very precious.

Our difficulties daily increased; the two sick ladies at Buyukdere were so alarmingly ill that the surgeon attending them required another nurse. We sent one of the hired nurses, but she returned the next day, having been found by the surgeon in a state of dead intoxication in the room of one of the ladies, then trembling between life and death; of course the nurse had to be sent home. One of the ladies of our party went to nurse the two others; another, whose duty it was, in addition to the care of her ward, to superintend the kitchen department, was suffering so from inflammation and weakness as to be often unable to leave her bed for a day or more.

The light conduct of another of the hired nurses, even at this time of distress, obliged her dismissal. The one who had been intoxicated was to accompany a lady to Scutari, from thence to take her passage to England. She went down quite quietly to the water's edge, put one foot into the caique in which the lady was sitting, and then jumped into the water, running the narrowest chance of upsetting the boat, in which case the lady must have been lost, as the strength of the current was fearful; the unfortunate woman was dragged out, and immediately went into what was apparently an epileptic fit. She was carried to her bed, on which she would not lie, but broke the windows, tore the matting from the floor and her hair from her head. Poor woman! she had before that openly avowed her belief that there was *no God!* After some days she recovered, was sent home, and, I believe, is now a nurse in a London hospital. Such and many similar tales could be told of those who came from and returned to nurse the poor of England.

March opened with variations of cold and days of spring-like loveliness. Once, as a great event, we took a walk to the Turkish cemetery. The lady superintendent, fearing our health would completely give way, desired us to do so—how we enjoyed the fresh air and lovely view after our long confinement to the wards!

Our next trouble was the sickening with fever of the third lady who had gone to nurse the two others at Buyukdere, and also of the nurse who had been sent to assist her. There were now at Buyukdere four in bed; the two first out of immediate danger, but in a most precarious state. Miss

Nightingale kindly sent a nurse from Scutari, for from our staff we knew not how to spare one.

It was a sad sight to see these three ladies lying in a foreign hotel, far from friends and home, and suffering under a deadly disease, their companions unable to be with them; but a merciful Father raised up help as it was needed. One of the surgeons of the naval hospital, Therapia (three miles from Buyukdere), attended them all through their illness—twice a day, sometimes oftener, did he come from his own arduous duties to their bedsides; he was not only physician, but, as they afterwards expressed it, "father and brother;" his kindness was beyond words to express. The ladies belonging to the naval hospital also came forward with sisterly kindness in this time of distress. One who had herself risen from a bed of sickness took her turn to watch at night by the bedside of those who were strangers to her.

At Koulali the work did not abate; as quickly as we sent home convalescents to England, so did others begin to pour in from the camp. The Irish soldiers now came down in shoals. We suppose this was caused by their constitutions being more inured to hardships than the English, and their having in consequence held out longer, although now worn out.

Oh! what grievous scenes was our daily life now passed among! The cases of frost-bite exceeded in horror all one had ever imagined. Dressing wounds was not our business; there were "dressers" who fulfilled this office; when the frost-bite had extended so far up the foot that it could not be stopped, amputation was the only means of saving life, and *it* even was but a chance, for their constitutions were so broken that many were unable to rally from the shock. At this time in the surgical ward were three men just in this state, Fitzgerald, Flack, and Cooney.

Fitzgerald had lost a foot, so had the two others, and some of the toes of the remaining foot. Cooney was about eighteen or nineteen; he was an Irish Catholic. Poor fellow! he suffered so much from being obliged to lie in one position that he was covered with sores. He was so thin his bones seemed almost coming through his skin; and his state was such that not even an orderly was allowed to turn him from one side to another; but the surgeon had to do it himself, and Dr. Temple most tenderly did it for him. Dr. Temple was one who almost lived in his ward, who thought no trouble too much, no time too long, to be devoted to his men.

Severe things have been said of the medical department of the army; and its members were, apparently, so despised that their work was taken from them in some measure, and put into the hands of civilians. No doubt some of the heads of the department who had grown old under the old system of military hospitals, and were unable to realise the necessity of a prompt and immediate change, were obstinate and hard-hearted. No doubt among such a large body of men many young and careless ones, unfitted for the awfully responsible charge then placed in their hands, were to be found; but in condemning such the merits of others should not be overlooked. Most ungrateful were it if the nurses should omit recording their experience of the much dreaded "army surgeons." So misrepresented had this class of men been that it was with far more fear of them than of the horrors of hospital life that the ladies entered the hospital. They were told to expect rebuffs, discouragements, and even insult. During a year's residence among them the writer and all her companions never experienced from an army surgeon other than assistance, encouragement, and gentlemanly treatment, and from many of them the most cordial kindness.

The tenacity of life in poor Cooney was wonderful; day after day, night after night, he lived and suffered on; growing weaker and weaker. How his piteous moans went through the hearts of his attendants, how terrible was it to watch the distortion of agony on his young face. Poor boy! he was very patient, and he said he knew "it was best for him, or the good God would not send him such suffering, and his trust was in Him, and he did try to be patient." We used to tempt him with the best of the little at our disposal, for Dr. Temple ordered him anything he could fancy. At length eggs, beat up with wine, were the only thing he could swallow, and until ten minutes before his death his nurse fed him with this. Death came at last, and he passed away as a child falls asleep, and with an intense relief did his attendants watch the calm, peaceful look on those features so long tortured with agony. One did not gaze long; in half-an-hour (and that was longer than usual) he was wrapped in his blanket, and carried to the dead-house.

Then there was poor Flack; he suffered too, we thought, the extent of human suffering. He was covered with sores, one foot off, and two toes of the other; he was ordered anything he liked, but in vain: he was in too much pain to eat, he "cared for nothin'—nothin' would save him." One day he said, "Tell ye what I could eat—a bit of apple-pudding!" But, oh dear! we thought, how was it to be got? how get the flour and the apples? and how get it boiled? However, it was made, but he could hardly touch it, though he insisted on its being set down by his side. Another man had the same fancy, and he declared it had "done him more good than all the physic." Poor Flack died one night—quite quietly, they told us.

Fitzgerald we watched by many a time,

expecting to see him die; he looked just like a corpse; his strength was utterly gone. Among so many interesting cases he was one distinguished from all others, not only by his patience, but his cheerfulness. He was an Irishman all over, always merry, and making the best of everything; his gratitude for being waited upon was great. Even when apparently in a dying state he would look up into our faces and smile. He lingered on, his doctors having no hope of his recovery; it seemed impossible he could rally from such a shock. However, he did; his improvement at first was very gradual, but three months afterwards we had the satisfaction of seeing him leave the hospital for England, though of course a cripple still, as stout and rosy as one could wish to see; his face quite radiant with happiness at the thought of going back to " ould Ireland."

Each ward contained at that time sixty beds, and to give an idea how crowded we were it is enough to say that the number was afterwards reduced to thirty. Each patient lay on a low tressel bed, raised a few inches from the ground.

The news of the death of the Emperor of Russia came upon us with startling effect. Miss Stanley went through the wards and announced it to the men.

"Long life to ye!" said many of the Irish, in a tone of congratulation, as though we had been the instruments of his death. "It is better than a month's pay!" said another, and "God be praised!" cried many a sufferer.

It was curious enough that the day of the death of the emperor was signalised by an earthquake of a very violent nature. That scene will never be forgotten by those who witnessed it. It occurred about three o'clock in the afternoon. The day before a heavy mist hung over the Bosphorus—a very unusual thing for Turkey. The hospital was shaken most violently; an instant rush was made by the nurses for the barrack-yard. Many of the poor patients jumped out of their beds, and, forgetting their sufferings in their terror, ran down the wards with fearful cries, and when the immediate excitement was over were unable to return to their beds without assistance. The clocks fell from the walls, and innumerable articles rolled about in great confusion. The extraordinary costumes of the patients and their extreme terror made the scene, awful as it was, almost ludicrous.

The lower division of the fever ward was occupied by Russian prisoners—such of them as were too ill to be removed when the hospital was given up to the British. They were attended by our surgeons, and we occasionally sent cocoa to them, but were forbidden by Lord William Paulet to visit them. It has before been remarked that the upper division of each ward was like a gallery with open palings. One of our patients in a fit of delirium jumped over these palings into the ward below, and falling upon one of the poor patients broke his collar-bone. The Russian never could be induced to believe but that it was done on purpose.

The cases of delirium among the poor patients were very trying. I remember one of the orderlies calling upon me to persuade a man to go to bed; his manner and tone were those of a man completely in his senses, but calmly and earnestly he assured me that he had committed the most horrible crimes, that justice was about to overtake him, and that it was useless for him to go to bed, as he was about to be plunged into a dark dungeon. He continued in this state for days, and could never be kept in bed except by force; and one day he leaped over the palings into the ward below and was killed on the spot.

One poor patient among the frost-bitten

attracted my attention by his constant refusal to take any sort of food, or to receive any kind of comfort that was offered to him. For a long time he would not speak, but one day, on my offering to write home for him, he burst into tears and told me his history. He had been attacked by frost-bite in the camp, and had been placed on a mule to go to Balaclava, there to embark for Koulali. The mule on which he rode was fastened to another, carrying baggage, which slipped and fell upon him. None of the party conducting the sick possessed so much as a knife to cut the straps which connected the two mules, and so for many minutes the mule lay upon him till a sailor, accidentally coming by, released him from his dreadful position. He was brought to Koulali hospital and treated for frost-bite, but when in a fair way of recovery from this, and with the prospect of coming home invalided, it was discovered that he had sustained a severe internal injury, from which there was but slight hope of his recovery, and the disappointment seemed to make his cup of sorrow run over, and he lay there in utter despair, not caring how soon death might release him. He was a member of the Church of England and had been religiously brought up and was one of the many who had enlisted in a moment of folly, and afterwards bitterly lamented his rash step. We became great friends from that day. He grew more cheerful, and willingly took whatever I wished him, and his gratitude was unbounded. He, however, became much better, but was then seized with typhus fever. He managed to rally through this also, and was able to walk to church—that night he was seized with inflammation and died two days afterwards.

These cases I insert as specimens of the kind then passing under our hands. The memory of each lady and Sister of Mercy would supply many such. Our occupations were so overwhelming that those working in the Barrack Hospital had not time even to visit the General Hospital, so that no more can be said than that this hospital proceeded on the same routine as the Barrack Hospital. The plan was for both hospitals to be served by sisters, ladies, and nurses, but of the two latter classes the ladies were ill, and the nurses either the same or dismissed for immoral conduct. The whole burden, therefore, fell upon the sisters, who admirably fulfilled their duties, giving great satisfaction to the Lady Superintendent and the medical officers. It would be only repetition to describe their work at this juncture, as it was like that executed by the ladies and sisters in the Barrack Hospital.

## CHAPTER VI.

Scenes in the nurses' room—An impertinent orderly—A minor misery—The strange interpreter—The hungry soldier—Miss Smythe's illness—Her death—The grave in a strange land—Miss Stanley's departure for England—Preparations for new arrivals—Change of quarters—Unwearied zeal of the Sisters of Mercy—The "Times" Commissioner—The dangerous person—Longing of the sick for fresh fruit—Mr. Stow's death.

EXTRAORDINARY were the scenes our one room would witness in the course of the day. The successive knocks at the door would bring a wild-looking Greek with a message, a grave Turk with another, a Scotch orderly, our Hungarian servant, his German wife, officers, French and Italian servants, an Irish nun, and an English lady.

On one occasion an orderly answered a lady impertinently in the ward, not choosing to attend to her directions for the patients' comfort. It was necessary to show the orderlies that we were instructed by the surgeons to carry out their orders, and, accordingly, when the medical officer in charge came his evening rounds, the lady reported the circumstance to him. We thought he would rebuke the man, and there would be an end of it. "Send him to the guard-room!" was the instant order. We were sorry, but of course thought the affair must end here. Next morning a tall corporal appeared at our room door demanding the lady's attendance before the commandant. He did not say what it was for, and she was quite alarmed and went in evident terror to the extreme amusement of her companions. The commandant received her with his usual courtesy, and assured her that he was determined no instance of disrespect or disobedience to the orders of the ladies should be suffered among the orderlies, and therefore he only wanted her evidence to dismiss the man from his post of orderly. As the lady passed from the " order room," through the line of soldiers on guard, she firmly determined that the orderlies must behave *very* badly indeed ere she would punish *herself* so again for their good.

One of the minor trials of life was our want of a female servant. With the severe pulls upon our time and strength, the labour of tending our own room was very great. One day we were standing over the brasiers, cooking in the yard, when a tall and remarkable-looking foreigner, speaking very broken English, suddenly stood beside us and began to make remarks upon the style of cooking, especially that of Henry, the sailor. Poor Henry's was certainly an original style, particularly in what he prepared for our own table. He always chose to think most of that branch of his business, and his delight was to send up *recherché* dishes in which grease was the largest ingredient.

The stranger informed us his name was Papafée; that he had a wife and child; that he was an Hungarian refugee; had been an officer in the Austrian service; had castles and untold riches in Hungary, but, having taken the side of his country and Kossuth, had lost them all, and was obliged to fly and earn his bread. His wife was a German, and could, he said, do household and needle work: as to himself, he could do everything according to his own account—he could "speak nine languages, write, keep accounts, shop, interpret, cook:" in short he was perfect.

Notwithstanding these perfections, as far as himself was concerned, we should have been unmindful of them; but we gladly engaged him for the sake of his wife, who, indeed, proved to us a treasure. Gentle, willing, and industrious, little Rosalie was a ray of comfort in our distress, though it was somewhat counterbalanced by her husband, who did everything we asked him with an air of infinite condescension, as if he were a monarch waiting on his subjects—to forget to ask him for everything before he went downstairs was an offence not easily forgiven. To want a spoon or glass more than he allowed would bring down a severe rebuke on our heads. He used to favour us with his opinion of things in general; whenever we offended him he would scold at us, not allowing our voices to be heard in self-defence, and, saying "It ees veri difficulte to please everybode!" would fling himself out of the room. It was, however, an amusement, and many a laugh did we have over his eccentricities.

Our invalids at Buyukdere still continued very ill, so did the sister and nurse of our party. Our whole staff now consisted of nine sisters, three ladies, and two nurses, and now Miss Smythe fell ill. She had been the stay of the lady party till now, never having suffered in the least from sickness: she had the charge of the fever ward, and her labours there were great and unremitting: I never saw a person more zealously devoted to her work. She, as well as the others, almost lived in her ward; her whole thought seemed to be for her patients—she fed them and waited upon them with most attentive care. She caught a violent cold so as to quite take away her voice. We begged of her to stay at home and nurse; but if she had, no one could have taken her place in the fever ward, and leave her men she would not. She went and stayed all day as usual, and would come back at tea time looking most worn and fatigued, and but with difficulty was persuaded to give up her evening rounds, which another undertook to attend to in addition to her own, while Miss Smythe went to bed.

After going round the long fever ward with night drinks, this lady was about to return home, when a poor man raised himself up and said, "Is not that ere lady a coming here to-night?" She explained the reason of her absence. "But is not she a cooking something for me?" No, she was not. "Well," said he, lying down again with a resigned look, "I be *very* hungry." The lady went back to quarters and asked Miss Smythe. She said he was very weak and ordered by the medical officer anything he fancied. It was so late the kitchen was closed; however, we contrived to take him a little of Mr. Gamble's soup, and he was delighted, and said it was the "beautifulest" thing he had ever tasted.

For some days longer Miss Smythe struggled on, till at length she gave in of her own accord, and stayed in bed one day. On that day letters reached us announcing that in a fortnight or three weeks a staff of ladies and nurses for Koulali would arrive. The news raised our fainting spirits—poor Miss Smythe especially expressed much pleasure. It was the last conscious thing we heard her say. Next day fever came on, and delirium as usual followed. A very excellent nurse attended her, and most skilful surgeons; all that could be done for her was done, and though we knew her case was a most severe one, still we hoped on, for up to this time all the members of our staff attacked with fever had escaped death, though all had hung for days at its very point.

On the 27th of March the chaplain of the Church of England administered the Communion to her; she was partly conscious at the time. Throughout her illness she had always displayed great patience; but she seldom spoke, and was constantly delirious. All this day the doctors spoke very badly of her case, but still we hoped against hope.

March 28th I was in the act of distributing the dinners to the orderlies for their wards, when the news of her death was brought to me, and it fell like the shock of a sudden death; and yet, such was our strange life at that time, I could not leave my employment, but was obliged to count out mutton-chops and half fowls till the hospital was served, and then went upstairs to the room of death. She died without a sigh, and in a state of unconsciousness. She had suffered from a malignant form of typhus fever, and the surgeons said that interment the next day was absolutely necessary.

Next day she was buried; the coffin was covered with a white sheet, the orderlies of her ward carried her body up the steep path which led from the hospital to the graveyard. All the convalescents wished to follow, but the cold was thought too keen for them. Ourselves and the officers followed the coffin, and we laid her on the green hill-side far away from the old churchyards of England, but we felt the ground was in some sense sacred, from the noble and brave who rested there.

A sudden chill came on us as we stood around her grave; the sun was sinking below the horizon, and lighting up distant Constantinople, the blue Bosphorus, and dark hills with its last glow. On one side lay in shade the Turkish Cemetery, the sad token that we were in a stranger land.

It was with a lonely feeling we laid her there, far away from friends and home, yet we knew God and His angels were as near, perhaps even nearer, to the exiles. She was not forgotten in Koulali. Deep was the regret expressed by the patients in the fever wards at the sudden death of their kind attendant. Many tears were shed for her; they spoke of her with real affection, and treasured up every instance of her kindness and self-denial. We immediately placed a small wooden cross at the head of her grave, and one of the soldiers carved her initials on it. We put it there to mark the spot till we could learn the wishes of her relatives on the point. At their desire her grave was afterwards covered with a stone monument, bearing simply the inscription of her name and date of her death. No word of praise follows, as thus it is ever meet the Christian should rest—he needs it not; for her the world's applause has passed away as shadows fleet before the sun. But we leave her in the humble hope that she will one day hear the words, "Inasmuch as ye did it unto the least of these, ye did it unto Me."

Two days after the funeral Miss Stanley left for England. She had already, at Lady Stratford's earnest request, delayed her departure for some weeks. Her departure was deeply regretted by all, especially the ladies and Sisters under her superintendence, who were now deprived of her gentle and impartial government; by the medical officers, whom she had promptly obeyed and cordially assisted, and by the patients who regarded her (as they did us all) with affectionate respect. The day preceding her departure Lord William Paulet's aide-de-camp visited us, to express Lord William's sense of the valuable services rendered by her to the hospital in his command.

The day she left us was very stormy, so that she had great difficulty in reaching the steamer lying in the Golden Horn. All the patients in the convalescent hospital able to walk came down to the quay to cheer her off as she left; the medical and other officers were assembled to bid her good-bye, and with many a heartfelt good wish and fervent blessing she was speeded on her way.

When she was gone our next step was to prepare for the new party of ladies and nurses. Before Miss Stanley left we had decided it was necessary to find new quarters, for two reasons: first, owing to the increased staff of medical and other officers there was not sufficient room in the hospital for their accommodation without the rooms we occupied; secondly, our health had suffered so severely from our quarters being in the hospital, that we felt to be outside its walls would be far more desirable.

The first house beyond the Riding School was examined and found to answer the purpose very well, except that the Turk who owned it objected to letting it even at the enormous rent he asked. It was necessary to apply through our embassy to the Sultan. Had we been French we should have gained possession in a few days, but British negotiations in the East are carried on with dignified slowness; so during the week that followed Miss Stanley's departure we were kept in daily expectation of hearing that the house was in our possession, and were daily disappointed.

Two days after Miss Stanley left one of the two remaining paid nurses sickened with fever; her companion was required to nurse her, so that the whole work of both hospitals fell upon the one lady and the ten sisters, one of whom was still dangerously ill. That lady can never forget the intense anxiety of that week, short as the time was. Every day precious lives hung in the balance; never can she forget the indefatigable manner in which the Sisters of Mercy carried on the work of the hospital. Already tasked beyond their strength, they willingly and cheerfully took the additional work which the departure, illness, and death among the lady staff had thrown on their hands, and so admirable was their method, so unremitting their skill, that no patient in the hospital (it may be confidently said) suffered from the diminution of numbers.

As the time for the arrival of the new party drew so near that they might be daily expected, and there was still no news from the embassy that we might have the house, matters looked serious. We had especially shrunk from bringing the new party fresh from sea air into rooms impregnated with fever. Of our four rooms, in one the nurse was lying ill of fever, in another Miss Smythe had died. However, there now appeared no choice. By applying to Dr. Humphrey, P.M.O., we obtained the temporary use of a room at the end of the new and unoccupied ward, situated at the extreme end of the building; this we made a dormitory for some of the paid nurses under charge of a lady, the rest we prepared accommodation for in our three rooms, the fourth having our invalid and her nurse.

At the end of this week a large number of invalids went to England, which somewhat thinned the wards. It was always a great labour when the invalids went, as we had to give them articles of clothing from our free-gift store. Sometimes we had not enough to give. There was a great want of brushes and combs among the men. Soldiers are generally supposed to carry them in their knapsacks, but almost all the sick who passed through our hands in the winter and spring had lost their knapsacks either in the camp or on the passage down; they were therefore quite destitute. We applied to Mr. Stow, the "Times" Commissioner, for brushes and combs, and many other articles we required for the men. He sent them immediately.

Previous to this date Mr. Stow visited us, informed us he had taken Mr. Macdonald's place, and was ready to give us any help we required from the "Times" Fund. We gladly availed ourselves of the offer, and we can thankfully bear witness to numberless comforts and necessaries supplied by the "Times" Fund to the sick. Mr. Stow appeared a person admirably suited for his post. He visited the hospital constantly and thoroughly, gaining a complete insight into its working.

There were other visitors to the hospital, who paid their visits once a fortnight or so, attended by a long train of authorities, and though doubtless it was meant for the best, yet it seemed impossible for these to gain such a knowledge of the real wants of the hospitals as a man who came and went at any hour and without observation. Great was my astonishment upon being told one day by a distinguished person that the "Times" Commissioner was a "dangerous person." I made no answer to the remark.

Living as we then were amid scenes of sickness and death, tending the wasted forms of those whom want and neglect had brought to this dire extremity, seeing as we *hourly* did the flower of the British army cut down in the prime of their youth and strength—as we saw those cherished in the heart of their country lacking daily the common comforts lavished on the sick of English hospitals—my heart was too sick and weary to enter into any controversy about the authorities and the "Times" Commissioner. I only knew one let the men die for want of things—the other provided them; the one *talked*, and the other *acted*. I could not help thinking that I cared not where the things came from so that they did come somehow; so I went straight to the "dangerous person," who was pacing up and down the barrack-yard, with an air as if he cared very little what people thought of him, and laid a list of our present wants before him.

"These things are promised," I said, "but we shall have to wait very long for them, even if we do get them at all." Mr. Stow wrote them down in his note-book; by that time the next day they were on the spot. This energy was one of Mr. Stow's characteristics. A thing once mentioned to him he never forgot, and never rested till it was done. He was particularly anxious on the subject of washing; it was a great evil, but at that time there was no remedy. Mr. Stow asked if we thought washing machines from England would be useful, but we told him there was no place to put them in, and then the plan would require much superintendence, for which we had no time to spare— we had not even time to search into the full extent of the abuse itself. However, his attention having been once drawn to it, he never lost sight of it. As time went on, we used to laugh among ourselves, and say, "Here comes Mr. Stow, and now we shall have something about the washing." If Mr. Stow had lived to return to Constantinople he would have found Koulali much improved in that as well as in all other respects.

The last visit Mr. Stow paid us was when the fruit was just coming into season, strawberries especially. We told him how the men longed for them, and he gave us leave to buy as many as we wanted. The new purveyor-in-chief being then in office, Mr. Stow seemed to feel his services were no longer wanted to the same extent. He said he knew Mr. Robertson would see that every requisite was furnished, and that matters would soon be on a different footing. He went to the camp, and among the many who regretted the untimely death of one so talented were some at Koulali, who will ever remember his untiring exertions in his country's cause, his extreme courtesy, and the kind and friendly manner with which he cheered on the sinking hearts that had struggled through that time of misfortune.

## CHAPTER VII.

New arrivals—Appointment of a Lady Superintendent—Illness of the last lady of Miss Stanley's band—The "Home" on the Bosphorus—Another earthquake—The plague of rats—The routine of an English nurse's life in an Eastern hospital—Mr. Stow's last visit—Commencement of night-work—Turkish ceremonial and harem hospitality—Dancing girls.

APRIL the 8th was Easter Sunday, but it, like joyous Christmas, fell strangely on us. On this day I sent Papafée, our interpreter, to Constantinople to be on the spot when the steamer was telegraphed by which we expected our staff of ladies and nurses, that he might go on board and bring two of the former to Koulali at once, in order that I might have an hour or two's warning to complete our preparations for the large party.

April 9th.—The morning passed away without Papafée's return, and I concluded the steamer had not come in; but at noon we were startled with the news that the admiral's small steamer, with "nurses on board," was alongside. I ran down to the beach and welcomed the party to their strange home and untried work. My first inquiry was why Papafée had not obeyed orders and brought me timely news. He, with violent gesticulations, excused himself, declaring he was the first who boarded the "Osiris," but shortly after he had done so there came a messenger from the embassy, desiring the lady in whose charge the party had travelled to come to Lady Stratford's immediately; this she did and stayed there to breakfast, and thus the delay had arisen.

The party had brought bedsteads and bedding with them from Marseilles, and this with the necessary number of boxes for so large a party was an appalling incursion into our crowded rooms. The corridor was already nearly full of presses, boxes, and some large cases of books, which could not be placed in the chaplain's quarters. There was no library, and the books were all carried to the chaplains, from whom we received them for distribution. The new party were twenty-five in number when they left England; five were left at Scutari, so that twenty joined our staff; they consisted of six ladies and fourteen hired nurses.

Before the new party could enter upon their respective work, it was necessary a lady superintendent, in the room of Miss Stanley, should be appointed. Up to this juncture the nurses in Koulali hospitals were nominally under Miss Nightingale's charge. She now resigned this charge, and we were informed of the fact by a letter to that effect from Mr. Bracebridge, and afterwards by a

## APPOINTMENT OF A SUPERINTENDENT. 155

verbal communication from Lord William Paulet, who said that now the appointment of the Superintendent of Nurses would rest in his hands, and that she would be responsible only to him, except in the details of hospital work, in which she was under obedience to the principal medical officer.

Three days afterwards Miss Hutton, one of the ladies of the new party, was nominated as Lady Superintendent, by Lord William Paulet.

Before commencing their work Miss Hutton laid before Dr. Humphrey, the principal medical officer, the rules for our work in the hospital, which had been drawn up by Miss Stanley previous to her departure. They were the following:

1. The nurses in charge of the wards should take care that the orders of the medical officers concerning ventilation are carried out, that everything should be clean and in order, and they should see to the cleanliness of the patients' beds.

2. They should see that the diet and medicine ordered by the medical officers be given at the appointed times, and that all their directions be strictly attended to.

3. The nurses will be in the wards when the surgeons pay their morning visits, in order to receive any directions they may give. They will be ready to wash or dress wounds, change poultices, apply fomentations, etc., as may be required.

4. The strictest attention is to be paid to the orders of the medical officers; nothing is to be given to the patients without their permission.

5. To each ward will be appointed a lady, a Sister of Mercy, and a nurse. The lady and nurse will enter and leave the ward together. They will visit the wards morning, afternoon, and evening, as they are wanted.

6. One lady will undertake the charge of the store-room, giving out whatever may be

needed to the ladies, sisters, and nurses for their wards. The same lady will also superintend the giving out of the extra diets for the patients.

7. Books shall not be given or lent to the patients by ladies or nurses unless received for that purpose from the chaplain of the communion to which the patient belongs.

The superintendent then assigned to each person her work, divided the wards between ladies and nuns, thereby releasing the overworked sisters from the double charge they had been holding for some weeks. This week the only lady left of Miss Stanley's band sickened, apparently with fever, and the superintendent had her instantly removed to the new house (which had been at last obtained), but only one room of which was ready for occupancy. The lady very much benefited by this removal to a room where she could be quiet and alone. The relief could only be imagined by those who had passed many months as we had sleeping and living in large numbers in one room in sickness and in health. The change of air or other causes, by God's blessing, gave the illness a favourable turn, and she resumed her work in a fortnight.

Ere this the necessary repairs were completed, and the whole body of ladies and nurses (with the exception of the sick nurse, who had had a relapse, and could not move), left their two rooms in the hospital and took possession of the house. It was a very pretty and convenient one. We called it the "Home on the Bosphorus;" but as this was rather too long a title it always went by the name of the "Home." Some apartments in the right wing were occupied by Dr. and Mrs. Tice; two small rooms were allotted by Lady Stratford's express desire to the senior chaplain of the Church of England. The apartments occupied by Dr. Tice and the chaplain adjoined our dining-room, but were otherwise divided from the rest of the house.

The house was built according to Turkish fashion, corridors on every floor, with rooms opening out of them; the kitchen separate from the house, adjoining it the bath-house. This was out of repair, and it would have taken too much time and expense to have put it to rights. The front rooms quite overhung the Bosphorus. We could see the water through the chinks of the rafters in the front part of the room. In a violent storm which occurred about this time, when the quiet Bosphorus lashed itself into fury, and when no caique would venture out, our rooms rocked as if they were cabins on board ship, and the new party were quite alarmed, and declared they expected to be in the Bosphorus soon; those who knew the climate assured them this was mild to winter storms at Therapia. Another earthquake occurred about this time, but it was not so alarming as the first.

From the first our house shared the fate of other Turkish houses—it was overrun with rats. They gallopped about the ceiling with a sound as of a regiment of horse. When we opened the cupboards we saw them disappearing into their holes. The devastation they wrought in the store-room was terrible; every morning beheld the lady who acted as housekeeper mourning over her losses and with no prospect of redress. At night they walked about our bedrooms, jumped upon our pillows, and quite broke the stillness of night. They would jump from stair to stair, sounding like a heavy man's footstep; they appeared to hammer and drive in nails, and saw and hack, till we could hardly believe they were only rats. Often did we rise, thinking there must be human beings moving about, but found it was only our usual visitors. One night a lady left a biscuit in the pocket of her dress, in the morning the dress was eaten through and the biscuit gone. At length we heard rat-traps were in the stores. We eagerly asked for some. The first night they were used three were caught in one room, and from this time the store-room was better guarded, as we put the trap on the hole and every night a rat came and was killed. But nothing was able really to subdue the numbers, and there is not a Turkish house which is not overrun with them. Those we caught were like English rats.

We will now give an account of the routine of our life. When May opened the sickness and deaths had considerably abated, and our system had become more organised and our hours regular. It should here be mentioned that on April the 21st three ladies and seven nurses joined us. Our numbers were therefore twenty-three nurses, (including the sick one), ten ladies, and ten Sisters of Mercy. The Sisters, as before mentioned, lived in rooms at the General Hospital.

At the ladies' Home we assembled at eight o'clock for prayers, read by our superintendent, then followed breakfast. At nine the bell for work rang. We all assembled; each lady called the nurse under her charge to accompany her to her ward, or kitchen, or linen stores (we never allowed the nurses to go out alone, unless with special permission); and in five minutes all the different groups were on their way to the hospital. At two the ladies and their nurses returned home, unless there were cases who could not safely be left to the orderlies' charge to watch them, and then the lady, or sister, in whose ward the case was, either stayed herself or appointed a nurse whom she could trust; but, generally speaking, we thought it better on all accounts to be absent from the wards for an hour or two.

At half-past two we dined, the ladies in one room, the nurses in another, with a lady at the head of their table. The ladies took it by turns, a week about, to superintend all the meals of the nurses. At half-past four the bell summoned us to return to the hospital. Some went sooner than this to the kitchen and linen store. At seven we returned to tea; then one lady—we took it in turns—went out with the nurses for a walk; now and then, for a treat, in caiques, to the sweet waters, or Bebec. At nine the chaplain of the Church of England came and read part of the evening service. Those who wished for it took some supper ere they went to their rooms. Of course such events as the arrival of sick, or extreme sickness in the hospital, would sometimes break the routine. So passed our lives for weeks and months.

We found our walks to and from the hospital rather inconvenient in the wet, and also the extreme heat, for it was on the banks of the Bosphorus that we had to walk under a burning sun. Umbrellas were at a premium, for those bought in Pera were made so slightly they were continually breaking, and then we had to wait till some one went across to buy some more. Those who possessed such treasures as English umbrellas treasured them with great care, but we had great reason to be thankful for the good health that we all enjoyed. We had only one case of serious illness among either ladies or nurses.

Exposed as we were to contagious diseases we greatly attribute this, under God's blessing, to our living outside the hospital walls, and also to the frequent exercise we took. It was often very fatiguing, after a long day in the wards, to escort the long train of nurses for an evening walk. They were rather exigeant in their wishes as to where they should go. Some wished to climb the hills to catch the breeze, while others declared they could only walk along the shore, while the oldest of the party (and rather a character amongst us) had yearnings after a krogue as she termed a caique.

A favourite walk with all was, however, to a neighbouring village called "Greek town." It used to amuse the nurses extremely to see the manners and customs of the inhabitants. On one occasion we found them all keeping festival; it was one of their numerous fête days, and apparently the day's celebration had something to do with a well possessing some medicinal qualities.

Not far from this was a pretty garden, where were assembled some Greek peasantry in their gayest costumes listening to music and merrily conversing with each other. The only remarkable feature in the dress of the Greek women is their head-dress, which is profusely ornamented with flowers, lace, and ribbon, a short gauze veil thrown over it. This is only among the peasantry. The Greek ladies are rapidly adopting Parisian style.

One day, shortly after we had got into regular work, our interpreter came running in and said, "Make haste, and you will see a sight which no English ladies have ever seen before!" Those of our party who happened to be at home followed him, and he took us into the next house, a few yards from our own. In the courtyard we found a large assemblage of Greeks and Turks, who all smiled and seemed very much pleased at our appearance, and conducted us into the house and into a large room on the ground floor.

What a picture it was! On the cushioned divan, which ran along one side of the room, sat three venerable-looking Imaums, in flowing robes, long beards, white turbans, and with chibouque. On their right and left, upon the divan, were seated a dozen boys, of ages varying from six to twelve, whose dress marked them of high rank. In a conspicuous position among these was a tiny boy, about four years old. He wore a little coat of crimson velvet, embroidered in gold; trousers and vest to match; a leather band, richly worked, round his waist, from which hung a tiny sword. On his head a velvet fez, beautifully embroidered, with a heavy gold tassel, completed his attire.

On a small desk before the Imaums were several large books in the Turkish language. One was lying open. Below the divan were rows of little Turks, all dressed alike in the coat and trousers and crimson cloth fez. They sat in rows on the floor like an English infant-school, and their little red caps made them look at a distance like a bed of poppies. Truth to say, they behaved a great deal better than the same number of little Britons would have done. Our entrance attracted their attention. Only for an instant they gave us a look, then settled themselves again. And now one Imaum called up one boy after another to read a sentence out of the great book; when he had finished his sentence all the school cried out, "Amen." At length the little boy whose dress we have described descended from his seat and stood at the Imaum's feet, then slowly repeated each word after the Imaums. He accomplished a sentence, a very loud "Amen!" followed, and there was a buzz and a smile on every one's face as if some feat had been accomplished. The child returned to his place and the other boys went up in turns for their lesson.

Now we were beckoned out of the room. Outside we found two pretty Greek girls, who by smiles and signs invited us upstairs to the hareém. We accepted the invitation, and soon arrived at the upper corridor of the house, from which numerous rooms opened. Here we were received by a number of Turkish ladies, children, and slaves, one or two other Greeks, as well as our conductress. Here we for the first time saw the Turkish women without their feridgees or yashmacs.

There was no furniture of any kind in the rooms but divans; the floors were matted and everything looked beautifully clean. We were seated on the divan and the ladies looked well at us, and inspected the textures of our dresses. They treated us with the greatest courtesy, and seemed delighted at the visit. Soon they brought us pipes and began to smoke themselves, and evidently watched to see what we should do. We accordingly made an effort at smoking, but thought it unnecessary to do more than smoke for a minute or two for politeness' sake, and when we laid down the pipes a general burst of laughter showed their amusement. Then came coffee, in tiny silver cups, and after this we rose to take our leave. But, no, we could not go. A small table and chairs were now brought in, and some Turkish sweetmeats and pastry offered. We were obliged to taste, or it would have been an affront.

After this we again prepared to take our leave. A great deal of talking went on between the Turkish and Greek women. The result was that when we reached the courtyard, where our interpreter waited for us, the Greek girls told him that the Turkish ladies hoped we would honour them again that evening and bring all the others with us. We said we were too large a party, but this made them miserable—so the superintendent consented.

At seven in the evening they sent in to know if we were not coming. At that hour a large number of the party were disengaged from work, and these went in. We were received with great delight; chairs were placed in the corridors, and they seemed hardly to know how to make enough of us. There were a large number of Turkish women now and many Greeks. There were several of the former strikingly beautiful, but a great number of the others had a sickly look, and evidently their beauty soon faded. Now they brought two large brass candlesticks, six feet high, with candles to match, and placed them in the centre of the room. We sat round by the wall on our chairs—the Turkish ladies in groups on the floor.

On the floor, opposite the lights, were three slaves with tambourines, who now began a hideous kind of music; the dancing girls entered and began to dance round the candlesticks. They danced very gracefully, but after a short time it grew very monotonous, although the interest the Turkish women took seemed not to flag for a minute. When this was ended they had some game among themselves, in which a key formed a principal part. We could not make out what it was, further than it was some joke about the key of the hareém.

At the conclusion of this game, some of the ladies approached us and made signs that they knew we were doctors, and they were very ill and wanted advice—they believed all English were doctors. Of course we made the most of our medical knowledge; sent for our little medicine chest, and prescribed some simple medicines, which could do no harm and which, with so much faith, might prove as efficacious as Parr's Life Pills or other wonders in England. After this ceremony we took our departure.

This festival was on the occasion of the son and heir of the house going to school for the first time; the father of the child being dead, the little boy was a person of great importance. We should mention that he was brought into the hareém and made a great pet of, and much admired. He was a pretty, intelligent-looking little fellow. The dress of many of the ladies was very handsome; silk, or gauze, with a great deal of embroidery and many jewels: the hair also much dressed, with gauze, artificial flowers, &c. Gloves evidently were considered the height of fashion among the ladies. They were only worn by ladies of high rank, who considered them a great ornament, and always liked them of bright colours.

## CHAPTER VIII.

Arrangement of the wards—Details of management—The jarring question—Better times—Gratitude of the patients—The drummer-boy—Yearnings for home—The old age of sickness—Our orderlies—A case of "delirium tremens"—The gentleman private—The English village-boy in an Eastern hospital—A last will and testament—The reformed corporal.

WE will now lead our readers through the wards, and endeavour to describe their arrangement and the order of their work. Ward No. 1 was called the "detachment ward," this meaning that which was occupied by the body of men stationed at the hospital. No. 2 was empty, the surgical patients having been removed from it till the horses could be dislodged from the stables beneath, which had rendered this ward very unhealthy. No. 3 was the fever ward; both upper and lower corridors had been filled with British sick for some time, the Russian prisoners (with the exception of two bad cases left in the surgical ward) having been removed towards the end of March to the arsenal at Constantinople.

No. 3 ward lower was under charge of a lady and nurse; No. 3 upper under charge of a Sister and nurse. The floor of No. 3 lower ward was brick, a large stove stood in the middle, and one table, which was of course not sufficient for the wants of the long ward. On each side of the ward, under the gallery, a wooden boarding was laid; on this were the tressel beds. The heads of these beds were open bars, on the top of which was a narrow ledge which held their medicine bottles, their drinking cup and dish (these two latter articles at least ought to have been there, but there was a sad deficiency in them). Over the bed was nailed a printed card, the blank spaces of which were filled up with writing; the information given on it was as follows: Name, regiment, date of admission, age, disease, religion—the last was inserted respectively, Church of England, Roman Catholic, Presbyterian. The benefit of this latter regulation was much felt in the hospital by the chaplains, ladies, and sisters, as they could thus each gain the knowledge of those belonging to their own faith without questioning the patients.

The card over their bed was not originally intended to bear this record of their faith, but the regulation was early made on account of the mistakes and almost absurdities which the want of it sometimes caused. There were few things so painful to us as the constantly being obliged to ask this question before we dared lend a book or speak a word of religious consolation to our patients, and it did them no good—sometimes causing a smile, and sometimes a look of annoyance, on their faces.

"I'm sick to death of that question," said a poor fellow very wearily one day to a lady; he did not the least intend it as rudeness, but the sergeant of the ward unfortunately took into his head that it was so, and after the lady had left he thought it necessary to report to the medical officer that this patient had spoken rudely to one of the ladies. The physician was much displeased of course, and immediately as a punishment knocked off his "extras," *i. e.*, reduced him to his original diet of bread and tea. The next day, in going my rounds, the poor man called me to his bedside and burst into tears, asking me if I could tell him where Miss ——— lived, as he wanted to ask her to come and speak to him. I replied that she lived in the same room as myself, and I would tell her to come; when she did so, he again burst into tears, and humbly apologised for his unintentional rudeness, saying, "It's not the extras I care for m'am, but having been thought to speak rudely to one of you kind ladies." She quite reassured him when she replied that the sergeant had been entirely mistaken, and that she never for a moment thought such a thing.

At one end of the ward was a long dresser, on which plates and tins, knives and forks, were kept; this dresser possessed cupboards in the lockers, two of which were assigned to the ladies' or sisters' use, to keep linen or wine and other articles likely to be needed in a hurry. The daily routine of the work was for the sister and lady to go round their wards with their surgeon and receive his direction, then give out the wine; it came in a large pail. Port wine was much used, one and two gills, respectively, being measured out; the extras were distributed. The regular dinner hour was half-past twelve, breakfast at seven, tea at four, but of course serious cases had to be attended to at all times, and food given to them constantly in small quantities.

The work was laborious no doubt, but now the agony of distress had passed away. Spring had come at last, and the woe of that terrible winter was already becoming like a dream. The party of ladies and nurses who arrived on April 9th saw scarcely anything of that sad distress, at least at Koulali. I am not acquainted whether the change at Scutari took place at the same time, though my impression is that it did; certainly with us at Easter the tide of death and disease suddenly turned after we sent home invalids in Holy week. We were never again overcrowded; mortality began visibly to decrease.

The unremitting exertions of the medical officer to conquer the diseases by skilful treatment, better food, and constant nursing, were blessed; and those who had passed through those dreary months felt as if they indeed heard the words, "It is enough, stay now thy hand." No one can imagine but they who experienced it the oppressive hopeless feeling the sight of that great mortality had brought, I suppose similar to that felt by those who have been spectators of the destruction wrought by the plague in foreign countries, and the cholera in our own.

To return to our subject; this emergency passed away, and our life was a regular routine of work and rest (except on occasions of extraordinary pressure) following each other in order; but whether in the strain of overwork or the steady fulfilment of our arduous duty, there was one bright ray ever shed over it, one thing that made labour light and sweet, and this was the respect, affection, and gratitude of the men. No words can tell it rightly, for it was unbounded, and as long as we stayed among them, it never changed. Familiar as our presence became to them, though we were in and out of the wards day and night they never forgot the respect due to our sex and position. Standing by those in bitter agony, when the force of old habits is great, or by those in the glow of returning health, or walking up the wards among orderlies and sergeants, never did a word which could offend a woman's ear fall upon ours. Even in the barrack-yard, passing by the guard-room or entrances, where stood groups of soldiers smoking and idling, the moment we approached all coarseness was hushed; and this lasted, not a week or a month, but the whole of my twelvemonth's residence, and my experience is also that of all my companions.

With some brilliant exceptions the manner in which the war has been conducted is a source of humiliation to England; but yet she has something left to boast of in her noble sons—brave before their enemies, gentle to their countrywomen—yes, many a time have our hearts bounded with joyful pride in our countrymen. Many instances of their nobility of character might be given; we select the most remarkable as we pass through each ward.

In No. 3 lower was M——; he was the only one seriously ill in the ward, so that a lady sat up one night for his sake only; this he knew, and he was quite distressed about it, and did nothing but cry, for he was very weak. "Really, M——, said she, it is useless for me to sit up if you are going to make yourself ill about it in this foolish way. I am quite strong enough to sit up till the morning, when I shall go to bed; but it is mere waste of time to come if you are going to cry in this way all night." "I can't abeer it," said he, "to see you running about and tiring yourself for me." At length she succeeded in quieting him, and when the morning came, finding him better, she left him.

Shortly after the lady of the ward came in to her daily work, when he eagerly enquired after his night nurse; and though he was assured of her perfect health and well-being, again did his tears begin to flow at the remembrance of what he had taken into his head to fancy was such very hard work. He was an orphan, and on his return to England had no home but the workhouse; his constitution being shattered, we fear for ever. Perhaps it was his lonely lot in this world that made him cling to us, and seem so astonished at any one caring for his comfort. It was the look of surprise on his face when he first came down from the Crimea at the least little act of kindness that affected one more than anything; he had evidently not been much accustomed to receive it through life, but he always said, with a smile on his face, that it was " all right—God knew best."

In this ward was Walter, a little drummer boy about twelve; he was a pretty child, with a remarkably clear sweet voice, and had been admitted into the singing class; he was very much spoiled by the soldiers, and had grown saucy and conceited. He caught fever, and came into No. 3 lower. When he was getting better he said to the lady,

"I have been a very naughty boy before I was ill, but I mean to change now. I promised father, when I came away, that I would read the Bible every day, and say my prayers, and I have kept my promise in a sort of way, for I always did it; but then I chose out the very shortest chapters, and said my prayers as fast as I could, just to get over it somehow, but I shan't do that again if I get well."

Afterwards he used to bring the lady beautiful flowers, as a childish mark of affection and gratitude for her having nursed him.

Another patient in this ward had a broken jaw, which had been struck by a heavy blow at the taking of the Redan, and, in consequence, though he recovered his health, he could not eat the usual hospital diet, and was entirely dieted from the ladies' kitchen with rice pudding, beef tea, arrowroot, &c. He was very anxious to be sent to England, but one day he said to the lady of his ward, in a melancholy tone,

"I shall never get sent home if you are so kind to me, and feed me up like this, for my arms has grown so fat; and when the chief doctors come their rounds to examine the men for England, they takes hold of them and feels them, and then they don't think I'm bad enough to be 'invalided home.'"

"Well," said the lady, laughing, "I suppose I had better leave off taking care of you!"

He did not seem at all certain whether it would not be better to starve a little, for the sake of getting home. However, at last his wish was granted, and he was invalided home.

He told the lady, the night before he set sail for home, that his widowed mother in England would pray for her.

The surgeons were of course anxious to keep the men in the East as long as there was the least hope of their recovery; but it used to be weary work to be kept waiting month after month, with their constitutions so broken and shattered, that, in spite of all that was done for them, both by doctors and nurses, they were obliged to be dismissed home at last. The thought of going home seemed to pour new life into them for the time. Many of them used to come from the Crimea looking so worn and so *old*, it used to startle us sometimes when we glanced at the card above their head to see their real age.

"You only twenty?"

"Yes, that's all," was the answer, "but we had a hard time of it up there!"

Our orderlies were a great help to us; they were always most respectful and obedient, though of course they needed constantly looking after. One of our nurses mistook their names, and always called them "Aldernies."

"Now, Alderney, run and get this beef tea warmed!"

"If you please, nurse, there's no fire, and the charcoal is all gone, and the Greeks 'as run over the brasier in the barrack-yard with their carts and 'as knocked off two of its legs!"

"Never mind that, Alderney, you can get a requisition for charcoal, and you can put up the brasier with stones, and get the water hot. If we want a fire we must have a fire, so that's the long and short of it!"

One day a man was brought in to No. 3 lower from the guard-room, where he had been confined for the night, in consequence of having been found drunk on duty. On being put into the guard-room those who had charge of the prisoners were so struck by the strangeness of his manner that they thought best to watch him; and fortunately they did so, for he had loaded his musket and intended to destroy himself. It was a sad case of *delirium tremens*—he never recovered his senses while with us. He more than once rushed out of the ward, managed to elude the sentries at the entrance, and attempted to throw himself into the Bosphorus, but our orderlies followed and brought him back.

When in the ward he was very quiet, seldom spoke, except to tell the lady that he was pursued by evil spirits, and had sinned beyond the hope of forgiveness; in vain she tried to cheer and comfort him. The chaplain, too, did all in his power, and some of the patients were very kind—trying to amuse and draw him out of himself, and to persuade him to walk with them in the barrack yard. He promised one of the lads that he would go with him to church, but when he got to the door he rushed back again, saying some one was going to kill him. Poor fellow, it was terrible to witness his remorse, and listen to his bitter self-accusations. We vainly assured him of the pardon and peace which he seemed to have lost the power of believing. Sometimes he would repeat the Lord's prayer after the lady, and listen to a hymn, and say it was very nice; but he soon relapsed into his former despondency, and the doctors, after trying all they could to restore him to health, were finally obliged to send him to England under careful charge, lest he should drown himself, as I fear he intended.

In No. 3 lower was also another very interesting case—a young lad, with whose quiet and really gentlemanly manners we were much struck. He seemed much superior to those around him, but was so reserved that he rarely spoke, though he appeared unhappy, and as if he needed sympathy. At last he confided to us his history. He was the son of an English gentleman; had been sent to school at Rugby. In a wayward moment he had enlisted and had left England without the knowledge of his father or his friends. After a little persuasion the chaplain prevailed upon him to write and tell his father the truth, and we had the satisfaction of knowing before he left the hospital that he had obtained his father's forgiveness. We believe he eventually went up to Sebastopol.

Another case was a young man with very bad typhus fever. He was not expected to recover. His mind continually wandered, but he was very obedient and docile. He used often to sing hymns, such, we would fancy, as he had learned in his childhood at some village church in England, for he was evidently a country lad. He was extremely fond of repeating over and over again to the lady and the orderlies that God was very good, very good indeed, and that he loved Him. He found great relief from having large lumps of ice applied to his head; he was very grateful, telling the lady that she was like a mother to him, and better than a mother, for what he knew. Much to her surprise he recovered, and slowly regained his strength. He was so childlike in his obedience and affection, that she felt quite sorry, for her own sake, to see him quit her ward for the convalescent hospital.

Another poor fellow came down from the Crimea, after some months spent in the hospital there, looking utterly shattered and worn out, and apparently about fifty or thereabouts, but on looking at his card we found he was only twenty. He rallied for a few days, but sank at last. The day he died he told the lady of his ward that he had a little money which he wished to leave to some friend of his in Ireland, who had been the same to him as a father. He had no near relations living. The lady asked the commandant about it, who said that unless he made a will his money would of course go to the next of kin.

The soldiers have now a little book provided for each of them by the quartermaster, in which they set down their accounts, &c., and in which are written several military regulations. At the end there is a form for making a will. The corporal of the ward wrote out, according to the commandant's order, a copy of this, and then the poor fellow was required to sign his name in the presence of the medical officer. But, alas! his mind was now wandering, and the death dew was standing on his forehead. He just rallied sufficiently, however, a short time after, to sign his name. It was so touching to see the eager way in which the trembling hand fulfilled its task. True, it was but a pound or so he had to leave, but he seemed so anxious to show this last little testimony of affection and gratitude to one who had loved him and had been kind to the orphan boy when father and mother were laid in the grave.

In the intervals of reason that last day he got the lady to write a letter for him to this friend, but she was obliged to finish it after his death; one sentence he bade her write was, "I have gone through a power of hardships up at the front." His worn face did indeed speak of a power of hardships.

He was a Roman Catholic, and the lady therefore requested the Sister of Mercy in the gallery above to come down and pray by him, which she very often did during his illness; he died very peacefully, while she was reading the last prayers by his bedside, and without a groan.

Another man was quite an example to his regiment for his good conduct and sobriety; he had attained the rank of corporal. He had a very pleasant manner of talking to his fellow comrades, and persuading them not to indulge in drink. He had been a long time in the service, and, his health being shattered, was very anxious to return home to his wife and child: but he always said, smiling, that he was ready to stay if necessary: that he knew for certain all would be right, whichever way it was. He told us so quaintly one day that it was "all through drink he came to be a good man." It sounded a strange anomaly, and we almost smiled, but the explanation followed. He had some years back, when a very young man, got into trouble through this habit; good advice was offered him. The captain of his regiment established a school, where those who wished to escape the temptation to drink which idleness offers, might find instruction and employment. He entered the school, broke through his bad habit, and said "he blessed God for the day he began to do so."

After his return to England he wrote the following letter to the lady of his ward:—

"Dear Madam,—With gratitude to Almighty God I arrived in dear old England once again, after a passage of fourteen days; beautiful weather the whole way; good accommodation on board the 'Niagara' for the sick and wounded. My pains are very troublesome at times. I am afraid I am worn out as far as military duties are concerned. It will be a great disadvantage to me to be discharged at the present time, but if it is so ordered I am satisfied with my lot. I feel it my duty as a Christian to submit to the Divine Providence of God, for I can truly say I have been brought by a way that I knew not, and by that same good Providence I am restored to my dear wife and family.

"I return you a thousand thanks for your kind care over me in my affliction. The Lord will reward you, because He has promised so to do. He seems to raise up friends for me in all parts. Please to tell Miss —— that I can never forget her kindness in giving me the advice and the address of her relatives. How many happy times have I spent in Koulali Hospital Church! the daily morning service was a blessing to me, and at the table of the Lord He was always present with me.

"You will please tell the Rev. Mr. Coney that I return him my thanks for his spiritual care over my soul there, and that I trust he will have many souls given him for his care and labour, although discouragement is around him.

"The joy and happiness of meeting my friends once more makes me almost forget what trials and hardships I went through. I am thankful my life is spared. I am content with my lot, but I am so much shook that I am happy to say I shall not be sent out again. I am at present attending hospital; I go for medicine three times a day. If the weather was not so wet it might be better for me; still I must not dictate to the Almighty what weather we are to have. And now, dear madam, you will excuse me if I have in any way transgressed in freedom in writing; my prayers shall ever be offered up for you, and all who belong to you, and you are a treasure to your family and the British army in the East.

"I remain your humble servant,

"——— ———.

"2nd Battalion Rifle Brigade, Aldershott Camp."

## CHAPTER IX.

The youth of the patients—An eccentric character—The general's visit—An idle ward-master—Care and tenderness—The Italian patient—The little sailor—Good advice—Letters home—The affectionate wife—Lower stable ward—Its arrangements—A member of the Evangelical Alliance—A case of frost-bite—The kind doctor—The sick man's home-sickness—Cases in the upper division of stable ward—Sergeant Everett—Case of delirium tremens—False newspaper paragraphs—Russian prisoners—Kindness of the patients towards each other—Newspaper reading in the Hospital—Men dressmakers—The untaught artist—A new Shelley—Cat and kitten—An instance of patience.

The extreme youth of some of our patients and their childishness was a great amusement to the orderlies, especially the Irish ones, who delighted in having, what they called, a spree with some of them.

"Now, Dick, my boy, what would you like this morning—a bit of plum-pudding or a few sugar-plums? ask the lady for some, she's sure to get them for you if you ask her."

"I'll tell you what, my boy, you better had stayed at home along with your mother than come a knocking out in this country; a bit of a chap like you ain't fit for such rough work."

One of the No. 3 orderlies was quite a character, and his eccentricities were a great amusement to us; his name was Rooke. Part of his business was to fetch the extras from the ladies' store-room for his ward; when he came back with a pail full of something in each hand, and his shirt-front remarkably enlarged from the bottles of soda-water he had ingeniously filled it with; he used to look of great importance, making as much noise as he could in setting them down, and calling out to the nurse—

"Now, nuss, here they be, and I hopes you 'as got enough to-day."

Whenever he had forgotten anything he had a peculiar way of rubbing his head and pulling his hair and trying to make excuses. He was a capital nurse, and full of rough kindness to the patients. He was generally so merry and full of Irish fun that it was a surprise to see him one morning looking sad and unhappy; but on inquiry we found that he had just received a letter telling him of the death of his wife, and asking what was to be done with his three little children.

He still went on doing his hospital work as attentively as before, but evidently with an aching heart. He said that he had known his poor wife ever since she was a little girl, that his mother and hers had lived in two adjoining cottages, and that they had been brought up and played together as children, and now she had died far away from him after a short illness. He used to save his money to send home to her and the children, looking forward with such hope to seeing them all again, and now he seemed utterly cast down, and the joking with his patients was at an end for some time.

At length, however, he somewhat recovered his spirits. In spite of his many good qualities he was remarkable for being as dirty and untidy in his dress as he dared without quite outraging military discipline.

One day General Storks and Mr. Stafford were coming round the hospital—everybody was astir—I think it was the general's first public inspection after he succeeded Lord William Paulet in command: such a clearing of wards and such a brushing up of everything took place. The lady at the extras store-room was serving out requisitions as usual when Rooke was the first on the spot to get his, and to her astonishment he was dressed up and in full regimentals. The expected visit had slipped her memory, seeing it made no difference to her work.

"Why, Rooke, what is the matter?" said she.

"They've a dressed me up to see that big man as is coming, if you please, miss."

Presently Rooke walked into his ward with a pailful of lemonade, and, setting it down by the lady, said—

"There, miss, now we'll give him a drink when he comes."

No sooner had the general's party left the hospital when Rooke the smart soldier returned, with evident satisfaction, to Rooke the untidy orderly.

No. 3 upper ward was under charge of Sister M—— O——, and also contained fever patients. It was a long gallery with tables and cupboards at the end. The corporal, who was ward-master, was idle and inefficient, and did not look after his orderlies, who of course became a riotous set. At one time the ward was dirty and neglected. Upon one occasion the ward-master insisted upon giving out the wine himself, instead of the lady; this was of course against rules altogether. The lady spoke to Dr. Beatson, who was staff-surgeon of the division. He instantly came in and told the ward-master to mind what he was about; if he disobeyed orders a second time he should go to the guard-room.

The superintendent, seeing the ward was one requiring peculiar care from the lady in charge, appointed Sister M—— A——, thinking this sister the best nurse in the Barrack Hospital.

In a few weeks the whole aspect of No. 3 upper was changed—it was clean and in order. The sister gained her usual influence over the orderlies—they loved and respected her so they would do anything to please her. In time she had a better ward-master.

It was astonishing the influence gained by the ladies and sisters over the orderlies. Without their superintendence they were an idle, useless set of men, callous to the sufferings of those around them, not trying to learn their business, which was of course new to them, and regardless of carrying out the doctor's orders when they could do so without getting into disgrace; but under the sisters' and ladies' hands they became an excellent set of nurses, forming that class of men-nurses of course essential in a military hospital.

A great drawback to this was, however, that often when one had a good orderly willing to learn, and had trained him into the way of waiting on the sick, he would be sent for to his regiment, his place supplied by another quite unused to hospital work, and with whom the teaching had to begin all over again.

One day a poor fellow was brought into No. 3 upper from a ship proceeding to Balaclava. He was an Italian, and could not speak a word either of French or English, and, although the surgeon of his ward could speak Italian, we could gather little of his history from his few dying words; for he was in the last stage of fever when brought into the hospital, and it was soon all over. He seemed so grateful for all that was done for him, and was so delighted to get a drink of lemonade, making signs to have plenty of sugar put in.

Another case up in this ward was a poor little sailor, who was also brought in from a ship going to Balaclava. He remained for a long time, and was eventually obliged to be sent to England with the military invalids. He was such a curious little man, very meek and quiet, but as frightened and nervous as a woman, always thinking himself much worse than he was in reality, speaking invariably in a tone of deep despondency, much to the vexation of the orderly who was especially directed to look after him night and day, and who was a great tall fellow, not apparently much afraid of anything or anybody. He was most kind and attentive to the small sailor, but evidently much chagrined at his want of hope and courage; he also seemed to think it must be very discouraging to the sister who attended to him, so whenever he saw her going up to the sailor he followed her and exhorted him very energetically to "spake up to the lady; don't be so down-hearted, man; spake up, man, spake up, she don't hear what you are a saying of; why don't ye cheer up a bit? ye'll never get well that rate; ye'll make yourself a deal worser being so low-spirited."

This was of course quite true, but the poor sailor did not seem much inclined, or indeed well able, to follow the advice of his soldier friend, though at last we did sometimes succeed in making him smile by declaring we would ask the commanding officer to make a soldier of him, and inquiring which regiment he would like to be enlisted in, picturing to him how brave he would look marching about with the coloured ribbons in his hat.

Writing their letters home for them was most amusing; very often they had not a word to say, but trusted entirely to the lady.

" What shall I say ?" we began with.

" Just anything at all you like, miss—just the same as you writes your own letters home. You knows how to make up a letter better than I do !"

" But how shall I begin ?"

" My dear Thomas," the lady writes on, hoping dear Thomas is well, and informing him of the illness and whereabouts of his friend.

Then she inquires what relation the said " dear Thomas " is to him.

" Oh, he's just my father, miss !"

She suggests the propriety of addressing him by his usual title.

" Oh, never mind, miss; it's all the same —it will do very well !"

One of the men received a letter from his wife, entreating him in the most broken-hearted words, to allow her to come out and nurse him—that she was utterly miserable, could not sleep at night thinking of what he was enduring, and so on. The poor man very likely felt more than he cared to express, but he chose to treat it with apparent indifference, and almost amusement.

"That's just the way women talks—they're always a-wanting to do unpossibilities. They fancies they can do anything! Oh, yes, they fancies it fast enough, but then, you see, they can't, so what's the good of it? I should like to see her come out here indeed! A pretty place for a woman by herself, and I shouldn't be able to see after her. She's much better at home, and I'll write and tell her once for all that it's impossible and no good whatever talking about it no more!"

Fortunately for the poor wife's feelings,

his arm was too stiff to write that day, as he evidently intended to send her a severe reproof for her folly, rather forgetting in his wisdom the deep affection and anxiety contained in her earnest pleading to come and nurse him. As the post went out next day, he rather reluctantly accepted the Sister's proposal to write in his stead, and she, of course, took care to soften the refusal as much as possible, and poor Mrs. —— was very likely rather surprised at the unusually affectionate letter she received from her husband by that mail; and we must hope it in some little measure compensated for her disappointment, though, doubtless, a few stern lines merely granting her request would have been far preferable.

Many of our patients could not read a word, and were delighted when we had time to teach them, or to read a few verses to those who were too weak to hold a book or read long for themselves. They were grateful, too, for slates to write and sum upon; but talking of home and bygone days, and then of their warlike adventures in the Crimea, was their chief delight.

Lower Stable Ward was the first of the stables turned into a ward. When Turkish stables, they looked as if it would be impossible to convert them into habitations for Christians, but when Dr. Tice was Principal Medical Officer he designed the improvement of this, and the execution reflected great credit on him: it became the best ward in the hospital, holding one hundred and fifty beds. It was large and airy, and had the unusual merit of being in the noonday heat of a Turkish summer perfectly cool.

The surgical cases were moved into it, and Dr. Temple was the officer in charge. This ward was entirely on the ground-floor, and very much wider than the other wards; therefore, though no division was made in the building, the superintendent divided the nursing between a lady and a Sister of Mercy, with nurses; the upper part of the ward, with its four rows of beds, was under Miss ——, and the lower under Sister M—— E——.

Under these ladies was one of the nurses who was a member of the Evangelical Alliance. She was an elderly person and very eccentric, but a very good nurse and a respectable woman, and gave great satisfaction to the Sister and lady under whom she worked. Sister M—— E—— always spoke in high terms of her usefulness and diligence, and she in her turn expressed the most unbounded respect and affection for the Sister, whom she called an "angel upon earth."

In Sister M—— E——'s division was a very interesting case—a Scotch Presbyterian of the name of Fisher. He came in to be treated with frost-bite, but the seeds of consumption were sown, and when the frost-bite healed he was evidently in a hopeless state. Never was the deceitful disease more plainly displayed than in that case. He lingered on month after month; now better, now apparently at the point of death; then the flame of life would suddenly spring up again, and a feverish strength made him imagine he was getting better. He wore away till his bones seemed ready to come through the skin. He was generally hungry and very fanciful.

There is something so affecting in watching by one whom one knows to be hovering on the verge of the grave, that every one united in doing their best to alleviate the sufferings of his last hours on earth. Dr. Temple stayed long by his bedside endeavouring to find something to ease him. Fisher insisted that no medicines did him good save those made by Dr. Temple's own hands, and the kind surgeon always humoured him, and when his rounds were over went regularly to the dispensary to make up Fisher's medicines, and he used to invent a sort of effervescent draught, which was to be sweet as well, and was Fisher's great delight.

By Fisher's bedside even the rough orderlies grew gentle; one in particular was a great favourite with the poor sufferer, and Fisher was never happy when "Joe" was away. Dr. Temple told us we might give him anything he fancied; nothing could do him harm. Oatmeal porridge he used to long for very often, and Sister M—— E—— used to make it strictly according to his own directions, for he was very fanciful. He was always longing for something or other, and as far as our means allowed he was supplied. Sister M—— E—— was most unremitting in her care of him, and the attention he required was constant.

Fisher was a singularly rough, quaint man, not given to many words of gratitude, but it was pleasing to see the way in which his pale wan face lit up when Sister M—— E—— made her appearance. His eyes followed her about the ward as she went to her other patients, and though he did not *say* much to express his sense of her services, yet a few words from him spoke a volume of the deep feeling that was in his breast. At last death came for him, he passed away without a visible pang, just worn out.

In the same division of the ward was Hickey, another most interesting case. He suffered from the same disease as Fisher, but its progress was far more rapid. Hickey was an Irish Catholic. His great longing was to go home; he was haunted by a perpetual fever to see his own green land once more, and when the deceitful rallyings of his complaint came his eye glittered as he talked of how soon he would be amongst his dear friends in the "old country;" and we who watched beside him saw in the very glitter of the eyes and flush on the pale cheek the signs that he no longer needed an earthly home. The goings to and fro of this world were soon to end for him.

To satisfy him, however, his name was put

down in the list of "invalided home," but ere the time for the departure of the band came the fever strength was gone, and the death-struggle was at hand. The disappointment was sore, but he bore it meekly: neither that nor his severe struggles elicited a murmuring word. He was a deeply religious man, and attended to the duties of his religion with fervour, and though the love of life was strong within him he was "content to die," he said, "as it was God's holy will," and when death stood beside him he passed as a child falls asleep and on his pale face was that look which clings to the memory for ever after, for it spoke of death without its sting.

In the upper division under Miss —— were many cases somewhat similar, but Fisher and Hickey were among the most interesting cases that passed through our hands. Another case of a very different character was in this division.

## SERGEANT EVERETT.

Sergeant Everett was a ward-master when the hospital was first opened. He had been at the Crimea and there lost his eye. He was discharged from this office for drunkenness, in which he indulged to a fearful extent. He belonged to the Church of England, and the chaplain was ignorant of his propensity, and Sergeant Everett got the right side of him, and the clergyman, being convinced he was a very worthy, religious man, appointed him Scripture-reader.

Everett had the Bible by heart. He could quote texts for an hour without stopping, and his power of talking on religious subjects was very great. He used to go round at night and read the Holy Bible to the soldiers, generally in a state of intoxication. Unfortunately he contrived to do it at the times the ladies, sisters, and officers were absent.

One night, however, he was reeling round Lower Stable Ward, Bible in hand, awfully desecrating the name of Christ, when Dr. Temple unexpectedly entered. The doctor immediately reported the circumstance to the chaplain, who of course dismissed him from his situation as Scripture-reader. A week afterwards he was brought into the Lower Stable Ward raving in *delirium tremens*, brought on by his habits of excessive intemperance. He was a fearful case to attend. He used the words of Holy Scripture in awful blasphemy; he would spring out of bed and knock down the orderlies, and it was with a great effort that the lady and sister approached him; but they had sufficient power to make him lie still and quiet while they were there: when they were gone he would recommence, and at night his fearful shrieks would be heard from one end of the hospital to the other. He required much attention, as it was necessary he should have a great deal of brandy given to him, and it was to be administered to him in very small quantities at a time. Often my hand shook at the glaring look of his one eye as he watched me measure out the brandy. At length he recovered and was invalided home.

To our astonishment, some months afterwards a paragraph appeared in the papers stating he had performed several feats of unheard-of valour at the siege of Sebastopol, which, as he left the camp immediately after the battle of the Alma, must have been done in his dreams. The paragraph stated he had received presents from both Her Majesty and Miss Nightingale. I am pretty sure he never saw Miss Nightingale at all, and his last statement regarding the ladies at Koulali was utterly untrue.

There were in this ward two Russian prisoners who had been too ill to be moved with the others; they were very gentle and submissive, and the cheerful smile with which they greeted us was somewhat of a relief to the usual heavy cast of their countenances. They were, while in the ward, treated the same as the other sick. They were the lions of the hospital, and a great many sailors and others came to see them, at which they appeared pleased. They talked a great deal to each other, and had a Russian Bible, which they read very constantly. Dr. Temple knew a little Russe, and when he made inquiries after their health in their own language their delight was very great.

This ward, at a later period than this, was principally filled with patients who had been wounded in the camp, and treated in the camp hospitals, and then sent down to Koulali for change of air and nursing before they were invalided home. The lady of the ward often used to remark their great kindness to each other; men who had lost an arm would be seen helping those who had lost a leg to walk, then these in their turn would cut up the food, or help in other ways those who had lost their arm or the use of it as the case might be.

The men were delighted with newspapers, and nine or ten would assemble together while one read aloud, and it was very amusing to hear their remarks on the things going on in the Crimea. They were so astonished and vexed at the attack of the 18th of June: "That was an unfortunate day, we did not gain any honour." One man comforted them by saying, "But no wonder it was not, *as* it was not *men* but *boys* that were driven back and behaved badly."

Some of the men were very clever at needlework, and hemmed dozens of pocket-handkerchiefs and towels to be given to the invalids when going to England, or those going up again to the camp. They also mended hundreds of the blue jackets and trousers, the outer hospital clothing. There was one man six feet two high; he had been wounded in the foot, and was unable to put it to the ground for a long time: he made a dress for an officer's wife in the Crimea, and made besides about thirty or forty sets of mosquito curtains.

We used to laugh among ourselves, and say this was the talented ward, for there were in it an artist and a poet. The artist's name was West, and he drew the picture which forms the frontispiece to the second volume of this work. He was a boy of nineteen, and he had really a talent for drawing figures; the one of the "Sergeant," in the drawing, is an excellent likeness. Of course the perspective of the drawing has been very much improved since it came out of his hands.

He was very diffident about his drawing, and for some time practised in secret, without ours or the surgeon's knowledge; but at length the admiration of his fellow patients was too great to be kept to themselves; the sergeant too evidently thought it a pity such a likeness of him should be "wasting its sweetness on the desert air," and so one day when the surgeon and lady were going the rounds, and standing by West's bed, the secret was divulged, and how West blushed as he exhibited his performances! When the ice was once broken and he really found we admired his sketches, his pride and pleasure knew no bounds. We supplied him with pencils and paper, and he whiled away many an hour by making sketches of his companions. He was "invalided home."

Another man was in the ward at this time, called Shelley, and he was the poet, and wrote really good lines on the different battles, which I regret I cannot give to my readers.

In this ward too was an orderly, who embroidered a pincushion with beads, and it was really beautifully done; he gave it to the lady of the ward as a token of his gratitude. The men who were nearly convalescent were often set to watch by the bad cases that required constant attention. There was one fine Highlander set to this duty; the patient in the next bed to him was very ill, and Miss H—— gave him in special charge to the Highlander at night. Going the night rounds once she found him lying on his bed, his face turned towards the sick man, and one eye open watching him, ready to spring out of bed at the slightest movement; the lady laughed and said it was just like a cat watching its kitten: this was heard by the others, and the pair went by the names of cat and kitten among their comrades for a long time.

There was another instance of the extreme patience of the men. One young man of the 9th regiment had been in the attack of the 18th of June; soon after it began his foot was shot off; the spot where he lay was so exposed to the fire of the Russians they could not fetch him in—he lay there the whole day—he tore up his shirt to stop the bleeding, and when the evening fell and they carried him in he was delirious from the agony he had endured from thirst; brain-fever followed, and he had to undergo amputation of part of his leg.

Soon after this he was brought down to Koulali. The movement again brought on fever, and made his leg very bad, and the surgeons found another amputation would be necessary, and they feared he would sink under this. However, it was tried, and he survived. His sufferings were very intense, beyond all expression, but he never murmured. We never heard him even groan except in his sleep, and then his moanings were piteous.

He was nineteen years old. His case was one which required most careful nursing; all the surgeons said, nothing but constant care and nourishment could save him. Great judgment was required in the administration of nourishment and stimulants, and great care also in the preparation of the first, which could not have been done except by the extra diet kitchen. It was pleasant to see his looks of delight when the ladies were waiting upon him, his eyes would sparkle, and many a time did he take the food to please Miss H—— which he would otherwise have turned from in disgust, having completely lost his appetite. At length he recovered, and was able to walk on crutches.

## CHAPTER X.

No. 4 wards—Sister Anne—Invalided—The fever patient—A case of delirium—A terrible cholera case—The convalescent's relapse—Bitter tears—The pain of gratitude—Habits of drinking overcome—A sergeant's letter to Sister Anne—Goody—His kindness and attention to the patients—The surly orderly—A ward-master under arrest—Fortune out of misfortune—More letters to Sister Anne.

No. 4 wards were exactly opposite No. 3, on the other side of the Barrack Square; its formation was exactly similar to that of No. 3. No. 4 ward lower was under Sister Anne (of St. Saviour's Home, Osnaburgh Street, an Anglican sisterhood). No. 4 upper was under Sister M—— B——. This sister was the one who had been so seriously ill with fever in the winter. She recovered and resumed her duties, and performed them with the utmost zeal and devotion; early in the summer fever again attacked her, and the second attack was even more dangerous than the first. For some days her life was despaired of, but she survived it, and on her recovery the surgeons declared it to be essential she should go home, as it was evident she could not bear the climate; and to our deep regret, accompanied by Sister M—— C——, she left Koulali on July 2nd.

All the other Sisters of Mercy were fully occupied at this time, and as the number of patients had diminished so as not to render the charge too laborious, both wards were assigned to Sister Anne.

This lady had a good deal of experience in nursing, and gave great satisfaction to the superintendent by her devotion to her work, while she was much and deservedly beloved by her patients. The surgeon in charge of the ward was Dr. Watson; both Sister M—— B—— and Sister Anne spoke in the warmest terms of his skill and attention to the men. No. 4 wards were always kept in beautiful order.

There was a man in this ward named A——. He was in brain-fever and perfectly unmanageable both by ward-masters and orderlies, and even by the surgeon, and they were forced to put on a strait-waistcoat to keep him in bed. Whenever the ladies came near him he grew calm, a single word seemed sufficient to compose him, and while they were present he would lie as still as a child.

A—— was a strong, powerful young man, doubly strong from the fever; his head required shaving, but the operation seemed impossible. No persuasion of doctor, ward-master, or orderly would induce him to submit to it quietly. They told him if he would have it cut quite close to his head it would do as well. No—he raved furiously at the idea. It was night, Sister Anne had gone home and the lady appointed to the night-watch came in, and, hearing of the difficulty, said,

"Now, A——, do let them do it."

"No one shall touch my head."

"That is very unkind of you, A——, when I have come so far to do it for you."

He looked at her and said,

"And please, ma'am, have not I come as far to let you do it?" and then, without another word, he submitted while she did cut off his hair.

A—— ultimately recovered.

C—— was another case in No. 4 upper ward; he was for a long time a patient from fever and diarrhœa, but recovered, and after several months of illness was discharged to duty.

A few days after this Sister Anne went up to the hospital at half-past nine one night, as she wished to see a patient who was very ill and decide whether he would require sitting up with. When she entered her ward she was astonished to find the state of confusion it was in. As she stood in the doorway a fearful cry of agony startled her. What was the matter? C—— had been brought in in a fearful state with cholera.

The information was given her by the ward-master, who was pale with terror and trembled from head to foot. Sister Anne begged him not to show such signs of dismay, reminding him that fear would spread the contagion among the others sooner than anything else.

She then approached C——'s bedside, and when she did so no longer wondered at the alarm of the sergeant and orderlies. It was an appalling sight. His face and hands were of a dark purple, both contorted with cramps, his whole frame convulsed, while at intervals he uttered a low moaning cry, between a scream and groan, scarcely like a human being. Sister Anne afterwards told us that so dreadful was the sight that her first impulse was to turn away, but second thoughts decided her that what he had to bear she could look on.

The surgeon entered and Sister Anne was very glad she was there, for brandy and other remedies were required immediately, and were furnished from her cupboard in the wards. The purveyor's store and the extra diet kitchen were both closed long before that hour of the night, and had they been obliged to send to either of these places for what they required nearly an hour must have been lost, and so violent was the disease and so rapid its progress it might then have been all too late. As it was, with the means they had at hand for immediate use, and the energetic application of proper remedies with the Divine blessing, although in the two days in No. 4 wards there were six cases of cholera in its most malignant form, they only lost one, and that one had been ill with *delirium tremens* for weeks previous to being attacked by cholera, so that when it seized him not a shadow of hope remained.

There was another case of a man named Ferguson. He came down from the camp in June, and entered No. 4 upper ward, was soon pronounced convalescent, and put on the list for invalided home. The day before the party were to go on board, the surgeon and Sister Anne were going round the wards; the latter observed a marked change in Ferguson, which had taken place in the course of a few hours. Whether his excitement and joy at the prospect of going home had produced fever, or whether he had caught the complaint from some one, we could not tell, but certainly the first symptoms of the fearful disease were plainly visible.

The doctor had stopped at his bedside, as was the custom, to say simply, "You go to England to-morrow," but his eyes fell on the fever-spot on his cheek. He looked at him attentively, felt his pulse, and said—

"Ferguson, I am very sorry, but I cannot decide upon your going to England till I have seen you to-morrow, or at least this afternoon."

Poor fellow, he was so disappointed. With an expression of intense anxiety and sorrow he rapidly assured the surgeon,

"I am quite well to-day, only weak; much better than I was yesterday. I am quite ready to go."

Sister Anne's heart sank as she listened to his words, for she felt assured his "going home" would not be to England; she was certain that he had no strength to resist the fever now preying on him. After the doctor was gone, in the bitterness of his great disappointment, he wept like a child.

Sister Anne reasoned with him, reminding him how impossible it was the doctor should have any motive for detaining him but for his own good; that he knew how kind the doctor always was to him, and surely he could trust her word. She begged him to keep quiet till the morrow, and not exhaust his little strength by sorrow, for she assured him if he were better to-morrow he should go. He grew calm and satisfied, consented to go to bed and see what to-morrow would bring forth. Next morning when Sister Anne entered her ward her first step was to hasten to his bedside, and it was touching to meet his look of quiet resignation. He said:

" Please, ma'am, I don't want to go to England. You were quite right, I'm not fit for it. I am so glad to be here while I am so ill, that you may take care of me as you have done."

Every care was taken, everything that could be done was done, but in vain. He sank rapidly, and in a few days was numbered among the dead.

M—— was another patient in that ward; he lingered for many months in dysentery, which was attended by violent vomiting.

This reduced his strength so much that at length he was so low as to be unable to feed himself, and for ten days Sister Anne fed him with a spoon, giving him food constantly in the smallest quantities. He used to entreat her to give it up, saying—

"Please, it's of no use, 'tis only wasting good food."

But of course she persevered in that and in everything else she thought could possibly conduce to his benefit, and she had the satisfaction to see her efforts, under God's blessing, crowned with success. He quite recovered, and was invalided home. On leaving the ward he came up to her, and, holding out his hand, said,

"Goodbye, ma'am, and God bless you; had it not been for you I never should have been home again."

Among the orderlies belonging to No. 4, was one named N——. When Sister Anne first took charge of No. 4 lower ward, N——

was much addicted to swearing—so at least she was *told*, for the men were far too respectful to swear in our presence. N—— was also given to drinking.

Sister Anne told him that if he continued in these habits she must ask for his dismissal from the wards. He admitted the truth of all she said as to the sin and disgrace, said he wished above all things to give her satisfaction, and that he would do anything she asked him to do. She said she expected him to give her his promise never to bring brandy into the wards. To this he agreed, and during many months he faithfully kept his word, infringing it only on the occasion of the battle of the Alma, when much feasting was going on, and an allowance was of course to be made, and he very much conquered the habit of swearing.

Another man, a sergeant, was led to leave off these two habits from Sister Anne's influence. When this man went afterwards to the camp he wrote letters which cheered the heart of this lady, and which, by her kind permission, we insert.

"Camp, Sebastopol, 7th Sept., 1855.

"Sister Anne,—I hope you will pardon me for not writing sooner, but the truth is I wrote a letter on the 3rd inst., but it was lost in the tent, and I waited until to-day thinking I might find it. The bombardment commenced on the 5th. The French opened a terrible fire on the enemy; ours did not commence in earnest until 4 A.M., the 6th inst. On the night of the 5th we set fire to the large three-decker of the Russians (the 'Twelve Apostles'), and to-day, the 7th, another large ship set fire to also. The 28th lost one man killed and wounded on the 6th inst. I do not know our loss to-day as yet, but we are firing very hard all day. We are to have three days' rations cooked in our havresacks to-morrow, and to parade at four A.M., which looks pretty like another attack on the Redan and Malakoff by us. We have no huts up as yet, so I think we will not require them now, for we are all determined to go into Sebastopol this time. We are getting fresh meat three or four times a-week, bread sometimes too, and potatoes occasionally, so we are not so bad off as you think; and, thanks to your kindness, I am better prepared this winter than I was last. Hoping this little account will not displease you, and you will pardon errors,

"I remain

"Your most obedient Servant,

"J. J———."

Goody was another orderly, and he deserved his name, for he was *good*. Everyone in the hospital knew him for his willing spirit, his sobriety, industry, and constant good humour; he was willing to help everybody, and grumbling did not seem natural to him, but he had such a perpetual grin on his face we thought he must go to sleep with it. Sister Anne talked to him one day about saving his money. He thought it was a capital idea, and he used regularly to bring it to her as soon as it was paid to him. By the time he left the ward it had amounted to a good sum.

Goody and N—— were quite exceptions to the general rule concerning orderlies; they could be left and trusted very much. Their affection and attention to their patients were remarkable; they were as gentle as women. Sister Anne suggested to them that in the case of patients who were much emaciated it would ease them to be lifted in sheets when their beds were made, and they never forgot the hint.

There was one orderly in this ward who possessed an unfortunately surly temper. He did not venture to show it to Sister Anne, but visited it upon one of her nurses.

One day when she went to the orderlies'

side of the ward requesting him to do some part of the work which was left to him to do, he answered her insolently, and said "she could do it herself." The nurse complained to Sister Anne, who said,—

"This is the second time the complaint has been made to me, and I have warned him that I would not again allow it to pass."

She sent notice to the commandant. To her astonishment, in a few minutes he appeared at the door of the ward with a sergeant, corporal, and picket of men. The commandant expressed his regret any soldier should have spoken rudely to a lady. Sister Anne explained that it was not to herself he had done so, but remarked as the nurses were under her protection it was her duty to see proper respect shown to them. In this he quite agreed, and trusted she would complain to him at once if any annoyance occurred, that it would be his pleasure as well as duty to assist her. He then asked if she intended preferring a charge against this orderly. She said certainly not. She only wanted him removed from the ward. This was done (the doctor's sanction having been obtained before the complaint was made), and another man made orderly in his stead. Thanking the commandant for his kindness, this formidable affair came to an end.

One morning on going to the ward Sister Anne saw something was wrong with her ward-master. He was one of the best in the hospital, sober and attentive to his duty. He looked very miserable, and came and told her he was a prisoner. She asked, "On whose charge?" "That of P——, an orderly who had told the commandant that Sergeant D—— had been out of the hospital after hours." She said, "Were you so?"

"No indeed. I was not in my own room, but I was not even out of this division of the hospital; I was in another sergeant's room upstairs spending an hour. The time passed on; I had not told the orderlies where to find me, but they all knew I was in this division." Sister Anne first satisfied herself as to the truth of this statement. She knew the orderly who had reported him was one who was about to be dismissed that very day for bad conduct, and who had an ill feeling against the sergeant.

She then went to the commandant, admitted the sergeant was to blame in not being in his room, but spoke of his general good conduct, the real loss it would be to her, and begged he might be pardoned. The commandant as usual listened kindly, but said it was now out of his power to do anything, as it had been referred to the general at Scutari, and D—————— must stand a court-martial.

This was sad tidings for the poor sergeant. He was in despair at the very thought, and begged her to use her influence at Scutari.

She replied that she could do but little there, she feared; she could only testify to his good conduct, and she was sure both his surgeon and staff-surgeon would bear her out, and that she would apply at head-quarters, and plead for his return. Beyond her expectations, the case was most readily attended to, and within two days she had the pleasure of receiving intimation that he was set at liberty without a court-martial, that he would have returned to Koulali at once, but that the adjutant having seen him considered him a superior man, and as he wanted a clerk for his office said he wished to retain him for that, and hoped Sister Anne would willingly part from him, as his pay would be treble to what he received as ward-master, and was besides a promotion.

She of course said she would not stand in his way, and there she thought the matter ended, but the best was to come. The following night Sergeant D—— came to the

"Home," and begged to see Sister Anne, then told her he could not bear to accept the offer made him without her consent and approval, and that he had told the adjutant so, for that he had received so much kindness from this lady he would rather give up the post than displease her. Sister Anne assured him she had no wish to stand in the way of such an advantage, and was very thankful it had happened. She was much gratified by the good feeling displayed.

The following letters will show more fully the man's character:—

"Adjutant-General's Office, Scutari, Nov. 25, 1855.

" SISTER ANNE,—I know you will be pleased to hear from me, and to know how I am getting on in my situation. I can assure you that I have made a good exchange; in the first place I will improve myself greatly, and secondly I am separated from a few people at Koulali who very probably would get me into another predicament. I am quite by myself and associated with no one. I am very thankful to you for allowing Sangers to go to my box to take some things out for me. I hope you are quite recovered in health again, and able to attend the 'hospital.' I will content myself with the hopes of soon receiving a letter from you; and trusting you are in the enjoyment of good health,

"Believe me to remain

"Yours, most respectfully,

" ———— "

" P. S.—Please remember me to F—— and ——."

"Soutari Barracks, 7th Dec., 1855.

"SISTER ANNE,—I received with deep gratitude your very handsome present, and shall ever feel the warmest sympathy towards you for your many kindnesses to me. I almost feel that I presume too much in addressing a lady to whom every one looks as a mother, but the poor man, although born in humble life, still has the warmness of feelings in his breast as well as the rich, and with it is therefore, Sister Anne, that I thank you again with all the warmth of that feeling, and shall ever feel it my duty to think upon and speak about you in the circle of my family and friends. I hope it will be your lot to remain long amongst us, administering the same great comforts and blessings that you have already shown. I feel quite comfortable in my new situation, and I thank you for the expression of your happiness on my promotion in the new line, quite different to the one I had before, although I would have been much happier had I stayed under you, but events occur and we know not until it is too late—but experience teaches us, and I intend to profit by it for the future. I beg of you, then, Sister Anne, to allow me to subscribe myself

"Your most obedient and humble servant,

"———"

## CHAPTER XI.

No. 5 Upper Ward—Civil and Military Surgeons—Dr. —— and his experiments—His advice to the Nurses—The stowing system—Miserable state of No. 5 Ward—An instance of Dr. ——'s eccentricity—Milk in Turkey—Short allowance—The sick boy on the banks of the Bosphorus—Dick and Algeo—The facetious orderly.

IN another ward in the Barrack Hospital both upper and lower divisions were under the charge of two Sisters of Mercy and two hired nurses. Both wards were under the same medical officer, Dr. ——, a civilian.

There were two civilians in Koulali Hospital, who held about the same position as staff-surgeon, and were much better paid. Their position was an anomalous one; they are nominally under the staff-surgeons and principal medical officer, but pretty much set them at defiance, and sometimes the assistant-surgeons were forced to be under them. The military surgeons of course chafed at the intrusion of these gentlemen, and I only wondered how they bore it with any patience at all, for they certainly did not do credit to the civil branch of the profession.

Dr. —— was a very eccentric person; he had many years previous to the war lived and practised at Constantinople, and had now come out, he said, from a purely benevolent desire to enlighten the military medical staff upon the true mode of treating the sick. We used to wonder whether the £2 2s. per day had anything to do with the benevolence.

Dr. —— chose to try experiments on these men. He said their diseases ought to be treated as the diseases of the inhabitants of Turkey were, by starving, quite forgetting the difference in the constitution and habits of the Turks, and also the labours our men had undergone in the camp, instead of spending their days cross-legged on a divan smoking a chibouque. But Dr. —— had a profound veneration for Turkey, its habits and customs—he maintained it was the best government and most moral country in the world.

He told us we were sadly wasting our time by not using the privilege of our sex in seeking admission into different harems and cultivating the acquaintance of the Turkish ladies, whose method of managing their households and children was so admirable.

In his ward the most exaggerated form of the starving system was established. How any of his patients existed we could not think—more died in his ward than in any other. Here it is but fair to state that some of the worst cases in the hospital were under his charge, and that the doctor himself insisted his ward was not a healthy one.

Nursing in his ward was a most miserable work: it was the constant witnessing of suffering and no means of relieving it. The ladies one and all declared the impossibility of working under him. The Sisters of Mercy made no remonstrance, and for many, many months patiently and devotedly did they fulfil their appointed duty, and that was one indeed arduous.

The comforts and encouragement which cheered on the ladies and sisters in other wards failed here. They who had been accustomed to courtesy and cordiality from the army surgeons were met with rudeness and constant hard rebuffs. In other wards if one committed an unintentional error in carrying out, or omitting to carry out, as the case might be, the doctor's orders, we were sure of being treated leniently and being taught how to do better for the future. In this one no mercy was shown to the offender.

The Sisters attached to this ward saw other wards gradually improving while theirs remained in the old state of dirt and neglect; they saw in the extra stores numberless comforts which they knew their men lacked and they dared not procure them for the poor sufferers. They saw the other Sisters and ladies counting numbers of convalescents in their wards, while their task was to watch the slow progress of disease and death in those committed to their care.

The depression of this was extreme—every one who visited the ward even felt its influence. The superintendent, who of course visited all the wards, often said she could not imagine how the Sisters bore up under their labour; but they never complained, they did all they were permitted to do for their patients, and soothed them with kind and gentle words, and they were not unappreciated.

"Never mind, Sister," said one, "we know you mayn't give us extras as the others do, but we like to see you smile."

An instance of the doctor's eccentricity may be given. He had a great fancy for putting his men on milk diet; he said all doctors had their *fad*, and that was his. If he had given them enough of his "fad" it would have been different.

In the hot weather it was very difficult to get good milk. There are hardly any cows in Turkey, and the milk was a concoction of goats' and asses' milk, with large proportions of chalk and water (beside it *London* milk would have looked like country cream), and for which we paid the moderate sum only of six piastres (twelve pence) the quart.

In hot weather this milk would not stand boiling; we tried heating without boiling, it would not stand that either. The first time this happened was at dinner time, when all the milk turned. A question arose what to send instead of the milk diets; a consultation with the ladies of other wards soon settled the point with them, but the Sisters of this ward dared not give an opinion; so the lady in charge of the extra diet kitchen sent a message to Dr. —— to know his orders. He immediately came to the kitchen and said,

"How many of my patients are on milk diet to-day?"

Glancing at the diet roll, the lady answered, "Eighteen: I was going to send you eighteen pints of rice-milk."

"I will have chicken broth instead," said he; "send me about one pint, or one pint and a half."

"You mean that quantity to each kind of rice-milk which is deficient?"

"No, ma'am," with great emphasis; "I mean one or one and a half pints of chicken broth. That, ma'am, will make four or five ounces' allowance for each man; and you may also send them each one a captain's biscuit," and he then departed.

A group of orderlies were standing by waiting for the ward dinners; when the doctor was out of hearing there was a burst of laughing among them.

"Well, I never!" says one; "if that ain't a rum notion though!—five ounces of chicken broth each for eighteen soldiers! Why 'tis worse than the camp and green coffee."

In the lower ward was a very interesting case named Algeo; he was quite a boy, and was a great sufferer, being covered with abscesses and quite unable to move himself at all; but Sister —— used to say she never saw him without a smile on his face, and when he slept it was touching to watch the look of calm endurance which was still there. The orderlies used to carry him out on his bed and lay him outside the hospital, on the shore of the Bosphorus, that the sea breeze might refresh him. All knew he was passing away from earth, and the orderlies and all were kind to this poor sufferer, almost yet a child, whose young life had been so strange and sad; first the battle-field and trench work, then the bed of wasting sickness.

Sister —— tended him with loving care, and he repaid it by his deep gratitude and affection.

An orderly in this ward was called Dick he was quite a character in his way, he was so rough and quaint, and looked as if he was just made to knock down a dozen Russians at once, but Dick was as kind to Algeo as if he had been his own child. Poor Algeo was so fond of him, and it was strange to watch the affection between the rough, hard soldier and the dying boy. His last agony came on, and just before he passed away he called for Dick.

"Come here, Dick; I want to kiss you, Dick."

And as Dick held him in his arms the boy died.

When the rough orderly told Sister —— of it the tears stood in his eyes.

This orderly was a strange character, he was so remarkably ugly, and was quite aware of the fact and rather proud of it.

"I be the best-looking man in the hospital," he used to say.

One Sunday I called to him as he was passing to take a message for me to one of the ladies. "You are the orderly from No. —— they call Dick, I think?"

"Yes, miss, they calls me Dick on week days and Richard on Sundays."

"Dick," said Miss ——, going into his ward to visit a sick man who belonged to the Church of England; "do you know if the chaplain has been here to-day?"

"I think I see'd him a knocking through the ward," was the answer.

Another ward was occupied by sick when

the hospital was crowded, but it was not considered healthy and was emptied as soon as possible and turned into a "detachment ward." Before we describe the other buildings of the Barrack Hospital we will visit the General Hospital of which we were very proud.

## CHAPTER XII.

The General Hospital at Koulali—Tradition respecting its site—The Turks' plan of building their hospitals—Dr. Hamilton—Nursing arrangements of the General Hospital at Koulali—Insufficiency of the Sisters' quarters—Their community-room—The Sisters' happiness in their work—The consumptive patient—Sugar-plums in the East—Great treasures in small things—Prevalence of chronic rheumatism—A private soldier's history—The large-hearted Irishman—A quiet cure—Convalescent yearnings for country rambles—The Sisters' influence over the soldiers—Vehement gratitude of the Irish—The convalescent ward—No nurses required for it—Afternoon visits—Its admirable state of order.

THE General Hospital, Koulali, has been before mentioned. It was originally built as an hospital to the Turkish barracks. Tradition says that on or near to its site formerly stood a church dedicated to the Archangel Michael; exactly opposite, on the European side, stood another church of the same dedication, for it was the old Christian belief that the guardianship of all the fortresses and buildings situated on the banks of the Bosphorus was entrusted to the Archangel Michael. It is remarkable that all ancient churches dedicated to St. Michael, not only in the East but in every country besides, are built on hills.

The Turks have one uniform plan for building their hospitals. Koulali was a miniature imitation of the large General Hospital, Scutari, and we admired the mode of building in some respects, and thought that with English improvements the Eastern plan would make excellent hospitals. Koulali General Hospital was a quadrangle, two stories high. It was built on the slope of the hill so that the main entrance opened on the second storey. Lovely was the view that one looked upon from the windows of the different wards; hill and water, trees and villages, in one of the loveliest turns of the Bosphorus. In the centre of the quadrangle was a garden which was planted with flower-beds, and it was the great delight of the convalescent patients to tend them, and cultivate flowers to give to the Sisters and ladies and to adorn their wards with. Here we could see the men, just able to crawl out of their wards, basking in the sun or trying their returning strength in walking on the grass. In the heat of summer a canopy was erected over the garden.

Round the quadrangle ran a corridor, which at the time we are speaking of was full of beds, out of which the wards opened. Each ward held about thirty beds. It would be needless repetition to describe them, as their furniture was similar to that of the barrack hospital.

The rooms were square, with no galleries

above—a stove in the centre of each. After passing through the upper corridor we descended the stairs. The lower corridor ran round the building with wards attached. One of these wards was not considered healthy, and was therefore disused when the press of work had ceased. A row of rooms ran opposite the main entrance in the courtyard. Among these were the general kitchen stores, guard-room, and room for storekeepers, servants, &c.

The medical officer first in charge of this hospital was Dr. Hamilton, whose skill and attention to the men were remarkable. Early in the summer he was ordered to the camp, and his loss was severely mourned by the patients, and by the Sisters of Mercy who worked under him. He was succeeded by Dr. Guy.

The nursing of this hospital was under the charge of the Reverend Mother of the Sisters of Mercy, she being of course under the orders of the lady-superintendent appointed by Lord William Paulet, but as the latter could not be on the spot so frequently as she was at the Barrack Hospital, both Miss Stanley and afterwards Miss Hutton wished the reverend mother to be responsible.

The mother had four Sisters, two ladies, and two nurses to assist her. She had long experience in hospital work, and possessed a skill and judgment in nursing attained by few. This hospital from first to last was admirably managed. The medical officers, both Dr. Hamilton and Dr. Guy, and the assistant-surgeons, fully appreciated her value, and there was a hearty co-operation between them. When the means of improvement were placed in her hands, they were judiciously used, and the hospital so improved that it became the admiration of all who visited it, and the pride of the ladies and nurses who worked in it, and we used to call it "the model hospital of the East."

At each end of the quadrangle were apartments; one side was given to the medical officers, the two on the other side to the Sisters of Mercy. One of these formed their community-room, the other their dormitory in which the ten Sisters slept for many months. Out of the community-room opened a very small one, hardly more than a large closet, which formed their oratory. When the soldiers attended their service they knelt in the outer room. When one of the Sisters was taken ill with fever the medical officers had her removed into a small room in another part of the hospital.

The superintendent deeply regretted the insufficient room given to the Sisters, while we lived in a large house; but the matter of hospital rooms was one over which she had no control

When the heat of the summer came on the hospital authorities took the matter into consideration, and it ended with five rooms in all being given over to the use of the Sisters.

Visitors to the General Hospital usually visited the Sisters, for they were universally beloved and respected, and they received all who called upon them with the utmost courtesy and sweetness of manner.

Their community-room was a good-sized and pleasant one, and furnished with the utmost simplicity—glass presses round the walls, which formed at once the Sisters' hospital library and free-gift store, as a portion of all free gifts sent to the hospital was always forwarded by the superintendent to the General Hospital; a deal table, a few chairs, and boxes for additional seats, completed the furniture of the room, which, though occupied by so many, was a pattern of extreme neatness, and the warm welcome we ever met there made it a pleasant resting place after ascending the steep hill from below.

Few of us had ever visited nuns before, and we often remarked among ourselves the bright, joyous spirit which pervaded one and all—their work evidently was their happiness, and we often marvelled also at their untiring industry. They never seemed to pass an idle moment, and in their leisure time they were always busy about some needlework or drawing.

The Sisters never left the hospital (except when business took them occasionally to Scutari) but in the evening, when it was considered necessary for their health to go outside the walls and walk on the hills around.

In No. 4 ward, upper hospital, was a poor boy who died at last in a deep decline. He was always craving for food, though it did him no good when he got it. He gave so much trouble to the orderlies, and from disease was so very irritable to them, that they often complained of his ill temper and ingratitude. But, poor boy, one could hardly blame him, looking on his thin, wan face, whiter than the pillow he laid his head upon, asking one minute to be turned this way, then that, then begging for another and another pillow till at last he got so many that the reverend mother, when going her rounds one day, inquired, with great surprise, the reason why this patient had seven pillows.

"Not one too many," said the poor boy; "I don't lay easy anyhow!"

The Sisters were very kind to him, and attended to his little fancies as if he had been a child. He was always asking for sugarplums and acid drops to moisten his parched mouth.

All these sort of things, sent out by kind friends from England, were of much comfort and were very superior to those made in Turkey. We tried in vain to get acidulated drops and good liquorice both in Pera and Stamboul, and when our English stock was exhausted we were obliged to content ourselves with the Turkish sweets, finding them better than nothing to give to those whose coughs not only kept themselves awake hour after hour, but their poor companions also.

This poor boy was as pleased as a child with some sugar-plums which Dr. Guy himself most kindly bought for him at the little neighbouring village. He used to keep them under his pillow, and the last thing the Sister did for him at night was to make sure he had enough to last till morning. His first request in the morning was generally to have a bit of buttered toast, and to have his wine and water made boiling hot.

It was not at all easy in the early days of the hospital to get either of these two requests attended to without considerable trouble, as there was but one large fire for the cooking of the whole hospital, and that at some distance from the wards; and with so many needing the Sisters' attention it was a long task having to go up and down corridors, waiting perhaps an hour to get a slice of bread toasted and a drop of boiling water, while others were anxiously waiting their return. But as soon as the Sisters had their brasiers this want was supplied, and great was the rejoicing.

None but they who have worked in the Eastern hospitals can imagine the unspeakable comfort a little charcoal brasier and small saucepan became, or what a privilege it was to get ten minutes' use of a fire.

The poor boy died at last, after weeks and weeks of weary, restless suffering.

One thing at this time the patients suffered sadly from was chronic rheumatism, and this often depressed their spirits more than anything else; they felt so hopeless of ultimate recovery, or of ever being " any good again to anybody," as they expressed it.

One tall, fine-looking man, in No. 4 ward, was often seen with the tears rolling down his cheeks. He looked quite well in the face and could walk about, but his left arm was utterly useless from long exposure in the trenches. He was blistered, leeched, cupped, &c., time after time, but it remained immoveable, and he was at length obliged to be invalided to England.

He was evidently so superior to many of the others that we were surprised to see by his card that he was only a private; but one day he related his history. That seven years ago he had been corporal of his regiment, and would probably ere this have obtained further promotion only that he had married without permission. He asked leave to do so of his commanding-officer, but was refused, and, to use his own words, " she and I were both very young and liked our own way, and so as we could not get leave we married without, and I was degraded immediately and have not obtained promotion since. She died," he added, "a few months afterwards." He related his story with a half-sad, half-proud smile, as if he thought the young wife now in her grave, far away in England—for whose love he had sacrificed his promotion—had been worth the sacrifice.

There was another, an Irishman, suffering from an apparently incurable malady in his limbs. He looked strong and hearty enough to have fought three or four Russians single-handed; but he was also invalided home. His joy at going back to "ould Ireland" was so great that he thought it advisable to drink his own health and those of the reverend mother and sisters and every one else in the hospital before his departure, so he persuaded one of the orderlies, who were sometimes open to temptation, to buy him some spirits; and when the reverend mother went in to give the travellers some clothes for their voyage home, she found him showering down blessings upon every one in such a very excited tone, that, instead of thanking him for those which as soon as she appeared he especially invoked on her own head, she very quietly went up to him, and, taking the large scissors which hung from her girdle, cut from his neck a ribbon, to which was suspended a religious medal often worn by the Catholics.

This silenced him at once: she left the ward with the medal in her hand, and poor Patrick was broken-hearted. He said "he'd have no pleasure in going home now," blamed himself for his folly in sending for the unhappy drink which had caused him this disgrace. In two hours they were to sail for England—what was to be done? One of the Sisters advised him to go and beg the reverend mother's pardon, and perhaps she would forgive him; he seemed cheered by the hope, took courage and went immediately, begged her very humbly to forgive him this once and he never would take a drop o' drink again till he got to the ould country. Not liking to let him leave the hospital in disgrace, she restored his medal and forgave him with many a word of good advice.

They often wished for a walk on the beautiful hills round the hospital, but Dr. Guy was afraid to give permission, as a few unruly ones might bring trouble on the rest. The innocent as usual had to suffer for the guilty, and that not a little, for it was most tantalising to sit at the gate of the hospital looking out on the lovely country beyond, longing, as the sick so often do, for the flowers and the fresh air, and yet not able to stir a step.

If those who nursed them could have put on the celebrated wishing cap of Arabian Nights notoriety, their patients longing for the green hills would soon have been gratified; but as it was they were forced to console them with the hope of future walks in old England: but it used to fret them sadly, and it was difficult to make them understand that it was at all reasonable for one man to suffer for the fault of another.

The Sisters' influence over the soldiers was very great. Earnest and touching were the blessings poured down on their heads.

"I shall be a different man when I go out of this hospital," said one.

"The prayers of my widowed mother in England will go up to heaven for you," said another.

The Irish were of course vehement in their gratitude, and very amusing besides. "It's myself that's proud to see you again this morning, Sister, and is not it myself that knows who's the best doctors in the hospitals now-a-days?" and some added, "What you gives us is better than all the doctor's stuff."

The convalescent ward, or hospital, as it was sometimes called, contained one hundred and fifty beds. As an ordinary rule, patients from the Barrack and General Hospitals were sent to the convalescent ward to perfect their recovery and gain strength. It was under the charge of a surgeon who lived in an apartment built on to the hospital; a small kitchen and surgery were also attached, so that the patients lived quite separate in every way from the other hospitals.

No nurses were required for this hospital, as all the patients were in a convalescent state. A few were now and then in bed, but if any serious illness arose among them they were sent back to the other hospitals. The men were, however, visited occasionally by the ladies and sisters.

We generally went in the afternoon, taking books and writing paper, and envelopes for their letters, and talking to the men, which they always enjoyed, for an hospital life, especially to a man, is a very monotonous one, and they used to appreciate what they called "having a bit of a chat."

The convalescent hospital was much admired; it was kept in beautiful order, and the men looked so well. It was in Dr. Tice's division as 1st class staff surgeon. Dr. O'Callaghan for some months, and afterwards Dr. Carolan, were the surgeons in charge.

Outside this hospital were always to be seen groups of invalids in their blue hospital dresses and white nightcaps, inhaling the fresh breezes from the Black Sea, and watching the vessels going up and returning from the Crimea. The rapidity and numbers of recoveries at Koulali were certainly greatly aided by the establishment and good management of the convalescent hospital.

## CHAPTER XIII.

Night work—Its origin—Its necessity—Sleepy orderlies—"All's well"—Drowsy sentinels—Our fellow watchers—Wood gathering—Gratitude of the Russian prisoners for a cup of tea—Heart-breaking work—The restlessness of cholera patients—A cheerful Scotchman—The long, long night—Violent storms—Danger of being shot as felonious Greeks—The fair light of dawn.

From the first day of our commencing our nursing at Koulali we much wished to have added night attendance as well as day. We felt that the want of this rendered our work imperfect.

During Miss Stanley's superintendence she had deeply regretted that it was impossible with our limited numbers, weakened by illness, and inefficient for the daily toil, to attempt it, except in such a case of emergency as that of the medical officer, whom we nursed at night.

When Miss Hutton had organised the work of her new party, she became anxious to establish it, and though the great sickness and mortality had passed away, yet we felt satisfied for a month or two there was sufficient sickness in the hospital to make this useful and beneficial.

While we were considering the expediency of the plan and the difficulties in its way, and especially whether the medical officers would now like it to begin (they had wished for it in the winter), this point was decided for us. There was a serious case of illness in No. 4 wards; one evening Sister Anne was standing beside the patient considering what she could do more ere she left him for the night, when the staff-surgeon of the division came up and remarked that this was a case requiring watching every hour of the twenty-four. She assented, and added, why is it not done? The surgeon asked if she would sit up? She replied, with all her heart; and she then went on to tell him what a strong wish for the establishment of night work was felt by all, and how gladly we would undertake it.

Arrangements were soon made, and from that time the "night watching" began, and continued regularly for some months. The first night the superintendent took upon herself, that she might more clearly lay down the rules to be followed. She then settled that a lady and nurse should take the office each night. We felt that the nurses could not be trusted without the ladies' supervision, while the ladies needed a companion. If serious cases of illness occurred, which required constant watching, the night nurses were to stay by their bedside; but the ordinary night work was intended for the benefit of those patients who ought not to be left for many hours together without medicine or cooling drinks.

There was a small room opening from our free-gift store, which was a shed in the middle of the barrack yard; this room was used in the daytime by the superintendent to receive persons on business. She gave it up to us for the night work. We entered it at 10 in the evening, and then went our first rounds.

In each ward there was a table called the Sister's or lady's table; on it we kept books and stationery, flowers, &c. On each of these tables we always found a little book in which was written the Sister's or lady's orders to the night nurse, as, of course, the regular attendants knew more about the cases in their own wards than those merely going in for the night.

It was a rule that one orderly should take it by turns to sit up at night; this, however, grew into the practice of his sitting up one hour, perhaps two, beyond his fellow orderlies, then going to bed in his clothes, which, perhaps, he imagined would keep him awake, but it certainly had not that effect, as he slept as soundly as the rest.

One night the night nurses could not find the Sister's book of directions, and there was a patient who had a blister on and they wanted to know what time it was to be taken off, and other directions about him; so their only resource was to awake the orderly to know what he had been doing with the Sister's book; the nurse touched, then spoke to him, but no effect, he slept too soundly to be easily awakened; at length she laid her hand on his shoulder and shook him and he opened his eyes, but was some time before he was sufficiently awake to answer her questions. He knew nothing about the blister or the medicine. However, we made him find the book, which he had been meddling with, and then we let him go back to bed.

Generally speaking, we much preferred that the orderlies should be asleep, for sometimes, after having been as we well knew fast asleep till we came in, they would stand up on our entrance, trying to make us believe they had been awake all night; and then they would begin walking about the ward, making such a noise; and they had a peculiar art, known only to themselves, of poking the candle just into a patient's eyes, so that we soon established the rule of their leaving the night watching entirely to us.

The first round finished we returned to our room, and remained there for an hour or two according as our cases required. Some of us were rather frightened at first by the quantity of great dogs who used to rush barking at them from the dark archways of the hospital, and also at the loud voices of the sentries challenging them from the entrance to each ward, with "Who goes there?" However, in a few nights we grew accustomed to it; we used to answer, boldly, to the "who goes there?"—"A friend." Then came the reply, "Advance, friend, and say, all's well!"

We pitied these poor sentries; they had often only just recovered from long illness, and were so weak as sometimes to be quite overpowered with sleep. Knowing that if they were found asleep they would undergo severe punishment, we always used to rouse them when we found them in this state, and sometimes they would start up, looking very much ashamed of our having caught them, or sometimes—and especially if they had been patients in our wards—thank us for our consideration.

One night we had just reached one of the archways and were about to enter, rather surprised at not having been challenged as usual, when the sentry, quite a boy, who had evidently dropped off to sleep, sprang to his feet and presented his musket, shouting the watchword at the top of his voice. We started back quite frightened.

"Why, sentry!" said the nurse, "are you going to shoot us?"

"Oh, no, miss," said he, lowering his gun, and looking rather ashamed, "but I thought I heard some one coming."

It was rather a break in their monotonous night-watch to see the nurse and lady going their rounds across the barrack-yard to the different wards, carrying hot tea, &c.

In the intervals of our rounds we occasionally tried to take a little rest, but it was a difficult if not impossible feat. The night-work altogether was something quite unique in its way, but there was little rest to be found, for our enemies, the fleas, had a decided objection to our doing so; they never approved of it much in the day time, but at night it was altogether against their laws and regulations to allow us to rest for a moment, so we walked up and down and did anything to divert our attention from the misery they caused us.

About twelve o'clock we lighted a fire and set on a kettle to make tea for our next round, and also a little for ourselves. Sometimes we had no wood and had to go foraging for it in the barrack-yard with our lantern, or by the light of the moon, which at times was dazzlingly beautiful, cheered by the songs of the nightingales, who warbled so loudly from the cemetery just above the hospital. When we had collected our wood we returned, lighted our fires, boiled our kettle, and had a cup of tea—all the more refreshing from having had so much trouble about it. The two Russian prisoners in Stable Ward were very grateful for a little tea at night, and told us so by expressive signs.

There were sometimes cases which required unceasing watching, and then some one was required to sit in the ward where the sufferer was lying; sometimes putting a piece of ice into his mouth every five minutes, or a spoonful of wine or beef tea. No words can tell what heart-aching work that night-work sometimes was, for though those we watched sometimes recovered it was mostly over the dying that we kept vigil in those long, dark wards, lighted here and there by a dim candle, and with three long rows of sleepers. It was indeed awful to stand by the wakeful, restless sufferer, to mark but too surely the gradual approach of that sleep from which there is no awaking on earth; to see the tossing of the aching head backwards and forwards, from side to side, and be unable to rest it, and to listen to the low moan which alone broke the stillness around.

This was especially the case with the cholera patients: restlessness seemed one of their sufferings. One poor fellow dying of one of the worst forms of cholera was always entreating to be taken away. "Take me somewhere, lift me up, take me away." All through one night this was his entreaty to the lady who watched him. "Pray, pray, take me away, I cannot stop here." She tried every means to soothe him, but in vain. At last she softly repeated in his ear the words of some familiar hymns, "Jesus, Thou our Rest shalt be;" or, "There is a happy land far, far, away." It pleased him and he lay quiet for a time and dozed a little; but soon awoke with the old entreaty to be moved, to be taken away. His prayer was answered ere next day's sunsetting; he was taken away, and to where "the weary are at rest."

One Scotchman who had lost a leg on the 18th of June was very wakeful at night. Sister Anne, when it was her turn to take the night-watch, remarked upon his extreme cheerfulness. He was in Lower Stable Ward. She said she was glad to see how he kept up his spirits. "Why, ma'am," he said, "it would be impossible not to be cheerful, situated as I am. In the first place I am going home with only the loss of a leg, and I am doing very well at present. I am free from great pain, and I ought to be cheerful and thankful when we are cared for and waited on night as well as day."

We could say with simple truth that many lives, humanly speaking, were saved by night-watching; for, had the care been relaxed, they must have lost at night what they gained by day.

"Oh!" some of the soldiers would say, "it makes the long, long night seem shorter when you come your rounds; when we cannot get to sleep we lie and watch for the sound of your footstep." "Will you have something to drink?" we used to say to those we found awake. "Yes, and God bless you, I am so very dry, my mouth so sore." And the Irish said they were "just kilt with the drought."

In the summer the nights were oppressively hot, and we often fanned the fever patients with large feather fans, and so soothed them to sleep. If any bad case of serious illness arose in the night, or if we saw any bad symptoms appearing or increasing, we roused the orderly, and sent him for the "orderly officer," this being one of the assistant-surgeons; for they take it in turns to be orderly officer, which is never to leave the hospital for twenty-four hours, and if any emergency arises the orderly officer is always sent for instead of the regular surgeon in charge of the ward.

Occasionally violent storms would occur in the night, the rain would descend in waterspouts like torrents, the gale rise so high that it was impossible to keep our lanterns alight, while the sky was so black we could not see the glimmering of the lamps at the gateways, and then we really did feel nervous about the challenging, for there were so many

Greeks who might have been prowling about the barrack-yard stealing wood or tools, or anything left about, that the sentries were on the alert in dark nights. However we never *did* get shot, and the storms did not occur very often. Soon after we commenced the night-work the weather grew settled, and it was charming till the intense heat came, and then the nights, though hot, were a relief to the broiling heat of the day. The moonlight nights were lovely, the surrounding hills stood out so clearly, the barrack-yard was still, and the distant Bosphorus was silvered over—all spoke of rest and quiet, save those many restless sufferers within the wards.

Beautiful was it to watch the morning break and the sun begin to rise—the "dawning of the morning on the mountains' golden heights;"—the hills, lit up with rays of gold, the bright-coloured clouds floating in the sky, and making distant Constantinople seem like a city of radiance.

The clear light air raised our spirits, but we were not unthankful when the wards were all astir and our night-watching ended—for we are forced to confess that the vision of bed, and a few hours' sleep therein, began to have more charms for us than the lovely view around us. We took our last round at five A.M. (the orderlies were now wide awake, and able to attend to their patients), and about seven or eight o'clock we walked along the shore, and reached home.

## CHAPTER XIV.

Shopping at Pera—An amusing half-hour's voyage—A miscellaneous crowd—Conversations with Turkish ladies—The beauty of the Bosphorus—The Sultan's lilac-coloured palace—The Sultan's usual residence—A marble mosque—Vicus Michaelicus—The principal French Military Hospital—Galata and Tophani—The Frank quarter—Scene of a massacre in the reign of Constantine—Constantine and his brothers—The tower of Galata—Liberality of the Greek emperors towards the Genoese—A street scene in Galata—Turkish porters—Swarms of beggars in Constantinople—A climb up the hill of Pera—The Hotel d'Angleterre—The Russian and Dutch Embassies—The shops in the Grand Rue—Ideas of the Turkish shopkeepers in respect to English wealth—Picturesque bustle in the Grande Rue—The British Embassy—A funeral procession—Death crowned with roses—Caiques and Caidjees—A row on the Bosphorus—"Sooltan, Sooltan"—Turkish Court etiquette—Sunset.

ABOUT this time we paid one or two visits to Pera for shopping. Pera is never reckoned as Constantinople. "Going to Constantinople" implies in Turkey that you are going to Stamboul or the ancient part of the city.

Our half-hour's voyage in the steamer was very amusing. We embarked either at Candalee or at another village about half-a-mile from Koulali, which was commonly called "Greek town," from the number of Greeks who resided there. Here we had to wait a short time for the steamer which started from Buyukdere, and stopped at these and other villages on the banks of the Bosphorus to take up passengers.

At the pier were always waiting a very heterogeneous mixture of individuals. Turkish ladies in their yashmacs, attended by their slaves, women of a lower rank with their bundles and babies, Greek ladies with uncovered heads, their hair wound round in long plaits and adorned with artificial flowers, forming a strange contrast to the others. Men and boys in their crimson fezs. The moment the steamer arrived there was a general rush. Politeness is a branch of education somewhat neglected by the generality of Turkish gentlemen, who mostly push and jostle every one before them, rush into the cabin and seize upon the best seats, where they immediately begin to smoke, and whether it rain or not never dream of offering their seat to a lady, however much she may need it.

The stern of the vessel is set apart for the Turkish women, and they are confided to the protection of a slave, who keeps a strict eye over his charge. We of course did as we liked, but generally followed the custom of the country, and seated ourselves among the ladies. We took a small Turkish vocabulary and tried to converse with them a little; they were charmed at this, and we always found them extremely affable and anxious to assist us in understanding their language.

How poor do words seem when we attempt to describe the wonderful beauty of that journey down the Bosphorus! Often as we took it afterwards it seemed ever new. The cloudless blue of the sky and the bright sunshine lit up each object with almost unearthly beauty. From Constantinople on the European side, and Scutari on the Asiatic, up to Buyukdere, the Bosphorus is one continuous line of houses, palaces, gardens, cemeteries, mosques, and minarets.

Soon after passing Koulali on the Asiatic side is a palace of the Sultan's, painted of a pale lilac colour. This palace is remarkable for its extreme gracefulness and lightness; it looks in the distance as if it were just resting on the water and a blast of wind would blow it away. It was said to be intended by the Sultan for the residence of the Emperor of the French, who was at that time expected to visit the East.

On the European side, among the numerous palaces the one nearest the Black Sea is a large pile of building with a beautiful terraced garden and fine trees (an especial beauty in Turkey, as excepting cypresses they are seldom seen). This palace was the permanent residence of the Sultan; he came from thence daily to his new palace a few miles lower down to see his ministers and attend to his state affairs.

About three miles below Constantinople, on the European side, is a mosque built of marble, and remarkable even among the many fine ones around for its exquisite carving. It is very small in comparison with the more ancient mosques.

Kurna Ishesmek is a very large village. This town was formerly called Vicus Michaelicus, because Constantine the Great here built a celebrated church in honour of the Archangel Michael which was destroyed, and then again restored by Justinian; after passing this the varied buildings of Constantinople lay spread before our eyes, and the steamer touching the bridge we are at Galata.

The two quarters of the city are connected by a bridge of boats, one end touching Stamboul and the other Pera or the Frank Quarter. Galata and Tophani lie at the foot of the hill of Pera. Galata is the worst part of the city, more filthy than the rest, and crowded by the vilest classes of people of all nations. The steamers all touch at the bridge, and it is necessary to pass through this Galata or Tophani in order to reach Pera. At the extremity of Pera on the summit of a hill, in one of the finest possible situations, stands the principal French Military Hospital.

The Frank quarter has little historical interest; almost the only fact concerning it in former times is the massacre which took place in the reign of Constantine IV., 668.

The emperor gave his two brothers the title of Augustus, and the title without the power raised their ambition. A body of troops took up their cause and approached Galata, making the following extraordinary demand:—"We are Christians, the sincere votaries of the undivided Trinity; since there are three equal persons in heaven there should be three equal on earth." Constantine pretended to receive them kindly, and invited them to a conference to discuss this novel view of earthly sovereignty. When they were all assembled, he thought the best way to subdue his brothers' ambition was to show them the bodies of all their adherents hanging on gibbets at Galata.

Such a tale of bloodshed in the far off times might be told to the traveller in every great city; but to their eyes all traces of such deeds have passed away, and the history of the past seems like a dream; but as one stands in Galata and looks around on those strange old houses, rugged streets, and fierce inhabitants, the time of conspiracy and massacre does not seem so far distant.

After passing through the streets of Galata, crowded with shops filled with the commonest Turkish and English goods and its crowds of sailors, soldiers, and beggars of all descriptions, we arrive at the tower of Galata, from the foot of which is a fine view of the city. This tower was built by the Genoese in 1216, at which time Galata first became a commercial town, for though it is a suburb of Constantinople it is also a town in itself. The Greek emperors gave the Genoese the privilege of being governed by the laws of their own republic, and they allowed them to fortify Galata with walls and towers which remain to this day. To their disgrace it is recorded that when the Ottoman army for the last time besieged Constantinople, the Genoese merchants, imagining that they could obtain good terms for themselves from the conqueror, assisted him in his designs. This baseness met with just punishment, and when the Greek empire was laid low the Latin colony also perished. The only remains of the Genoese are a church and monastery of Dominican friars.

Only one mosque is to be found at Galata. There are a great many Greek and Armenian churches. The numerous warehouses in Galata are built of stone to preserve them from fire, but the houses, as usual, are of wood.

One part of Galata is very narrow and particularly crowded; as we were slowly threading our way along a yell was heard, and there appeared coming into the midst of us a huge cart drawn by bullocks and loaded with baggage, violently forcing its way along utterly regardless what became of the crowd. How we escaped being crushed we scarcely knew; we were pushed into a barber's shop, where the barber and his customer just looked up and then continued their respective employments—the one of shaving, the other of smoking—not at all caring apparently whether we were crushed or not. When the araba had passed we proceeded on our way, and though not again placed in such danger, we were often obliged to take refuge in shops when yells or howls warned us a "hamel" was at hand.

Hamel is the Turkish for porter. These men seem capable of carrying weights far beyond the strength of an Englishman, though their wretched, distorted-looking figures are very different to the fine stalwart porters on our railways. The hamels always look as if they were bent double; on their backs they first fasten a piece of wood, on which they lay their heavy burdens, and they then tramp on caring for nothing that comes in their way, apparently as insensible to all around as if they were beasts of burden. One can hardly believe they are human beings, and the frightful yells they utter help to increase this feeling. Now and then, from extremity of fatigue, they halt and stooping down to the ground rest their burdens and themselves, then on they push again with renewed cries.

Beggars abound in Constantinople, and they present pictures of squalid misery, dirt, rags, and disease, unequalled in any city in the world. They are sights from which one involuntarily turns away. At Tophani there is a market for fruit and vegetables; among the former there were thousands of melons; they are nearly all water melons and taste like cucumbers. The heaps of fruit and vegetables are very well arranged and have a pretty effect. In the centre of the market-place is a beautiful fountain; it is of white marble, the roof slopes, and it is decorated with scriptural devices and sentences from the Koran.

Most people embark here for Scutari and the villages on the Bosphorus, preferring it to the din and bustle that goes on at Galata bridge. Tophani is quite bad enough in this way, but a few degrees better than Galata. Weary work is it after passing through Galata to climb the hill of Pera, especially on a hot summer's day; no shade to be found from the broiling sun. There is no pavement, or worse than none, for stones intended for paving are scattered about in all directions as though, as some one described it, they had tumbled suddenly out of a cart.

At the summit of the hill we found ourselves in the "Grande Rue." Here are the shops and the hotels. The Hotel d'Angleterre, generally spoken of as Missiri's, which can be known at once by the group of English gentlemen lounging about, whose costumes are of an extraordinary description—each one appearing to adopt something perfectly unique. An English gentleman is seldom seen in Pera without a white covering on his hat, or a white scarf round his wideawake.

Then come the Russian and Dutch embassies, and further on, beyond the extreme end of the "Grande Rue," the British embassy, and beyond that again, in a commanding situation, the principal French hospital. In the "Grande Rue" stands the Russian embassy—a very fine building now occupied as a French hospital.

The shops in the "Grande Rue" are kept either by French, or Greeks who can speak the French language. Here can be bought inferior French or English goods at an enormous price. A curious spirit of independence exists among the Pera shopkeepers. They do not in the least care whether you buy or not, and if one walks in and asks for a dress, one or two perhaps are laid down for your inspection, and if you do not like them you may go without. It is in vain to point to others you may see in the distance, you will not have a nearer view. The French as well as Greeks always ask exorbitant prices for their goods, and expect to be beaten down, taking at last nearly double what the article would be worth at home. Of course, the immense influx both of French and English into Pera, owing to the war, has much increased this spirit of independence and extortion among the shopkeepers, as they are pretty certain of finding customers for their goods sooner or later, and many to whom money is little or no object.

The general idea of the shopkeepers in Turkey is that the English are extremely rich, and only want an opportunity of spending their money which they have no objection to afford them. Another annoyance is that one can seldom get two articles of different sorts in one shop; you buy a dress, and want ribbon or braid to match—you must go to another shop. A pair of gloves, you must go elsewhere; blonde or net, they do not keep it, and so you are sent about from one shop to another till your patience is fairly exhausted. A common reel of English sewing cotton is a luxury rarely to be obtained.

Most of the English considered going to Pera a sort of punishment. It was indeed very fatiguing, but we thought still there was much enjoyment. The "Grande Rue" was like an ever moving picture. The narrow street was crowded with foot passengers, every now and then driven into doorways to save themselves from being run over by horsemen, Turkish carriages, or "hamels." Walking along, one met with every imaginable costume—now a Turk, then a Greek, next a French lady in full Parisian costume, French officers, English and Sardinian ditto, English, French, and Sardinian soldiers; a pasha on horseback, with his train; a group of Turkish women; another of Greek ladies; a Greek priest in flowing robes, long beard, and square cap; a Greek Catholic priest, distinguished from the other by the black gauze veil thrown over his cap; an Armenian priest in dark brown robes; a group of French clergy; an English chaplain; a *Sœur de la Charité*; a group of English sailors—so went the scene, so ran the din of many tongues.

Passing up the "Grande Rue" we reached the British embassy, which is a large mansion standing on an eminence and commanding a magnificent view; just at its foot lies a Turkish cemetery, with its attendant cypresses. The Golden Horn, the first windings of the Bosphorus, the Sea of Marmora, the distant range of mountains, Scutari, with its hospitals, all lie spread before the eye that gazes out of the embassy windows. Strange indeed must it have seemed to its occupants looking down from their palace over the fair view before them upon the abode of suffering, where the pride of the land they represented were dying of pestilence. What wildest romance could have imagined the change a few months had brought? Once no bitter feelings of a nation's humiliation mingled with the sight—but now, who shall from that residence ever gaze unmoved on the spot where so many British soldiers have suffered—on the ground where so many have lain down to their last rest?

The embassy is a fine building, standing in grounds of its own. On our return from thence we were proceeding down a narrow street which led into the "Grande Rue," when the dismal sound which the Greeks make in chanting struck on our ears. We saw a procession in the distance, and we squeezed ourselves against the walls as best we might to let it pass. Boys bearing tapers came first, then priests; followed by a bier, on which was laid the body of a young girl. The corpse was uncovered, that all might gaze on it, and strewn over with flowers; the pale, marble-like beauty of her face contrasted with the freshness of the roses, a chaplet of which crowned her head. A few hours only has she ceased to breathe, yet so soon are they bearing her to her last resting-place on earth; and the young face, from which life has but just fled, must in so sadly brief a period be shut out from the gaze of those who have loved it. It is this necessity for almost immediate interment after death which makes it so doubly painful to witness it in Turkey.

Illness, death, and burial follow each other in such rapid succession, that to the survivors it must often seem like a dream rather than a reality, that the joy of their homes and the sunshine of their hearts are gone from their gaze for ever in this world. More boys with tapers followed the bier, and then came the mourners. As they passed into the distance the chant sounded like a wail, and strangely indeed in that crowded city on that bright summer's day, did the passing sight of the calm face of the dead fall upon one's heart.

Descending from Pera we took the turn leading to Tophani, and thus escaped the disagreeables of passing through Galata. At Tophani pier (if such a name can be given to the construction of a few half-broken planks) we found many caiques lying, and were assailed as usual by the shrieks of caidjees, some pulling one's cloak to induce one to get into their caique. We were thankful when our interpreter had settled the question of fares, our next feat was to jump from the crazy pier into the middle of the caique, so as to keep the balance of the boat—then to settle down on the cushions at the bottom, and so lying full length, the caidjee pushed off and wound his way marvellously among the multitude of other craft which completely covered the water round the pier. This was no easy matter owing to the enormous quantities of boats and caiques surrounding us. It has been estimated that the number of caiques plying on the Bosphorus counts from eighty thousand and upwards.

At last we were free and swiftly we glided onwards past the great ships lying at anchor off Tophani—past palace and mosque and garden down the sunny Bosphorus, watching the different caiques as they glided by—now filled with Turkish women, their bright eyes glancing at the strangers from beneath their yashmacs—now a boat full of laughing Greek girls—now a grave Turk alone with his chibouque and his slaves—now one full of European gentlemen, whose costumes were quite as remarkable, and bore almost as little likeness to home as the Turks themselves. "Sooltan, Sooltan," says the caidjee. We were passing his new palace, and he was about to enter. Our caidjee rests on his oars respectfully till the monarch disembarks. The Royal caique touches the marble steps, the iron gates are wide open, the twelve rowers, all dressed in white, stand up, their hands hanging down straight by their sides—the attendants do so likewise.

No one assists the Sultan to rise or step from his caique. The slight, feeble-looking man walks slowly up the marble steps and pathway leading to his palace. His loose great coat and crimson fez do not distinguish him from a pasha. He opens the door himself and walks quietly in; not till he is fairly out of sight do the attendants move from their statue-like quietude and prepare to follow their master. Such is Turkish court etiquette.

Now we glide on, and the sun has gone down and the delicious breeze from the Black Sea blows upon us, and we are silent and look around. The last rays of the setting sun are lighting up for a few last minutes mosque, dome, and minaret, and village, and the many sombre groups of cypresses on either bank, and in the distance the hospital of Koulali, the bright red colour of its walls standing out against the dark hills beyond.

And now the sun sinks below the horizon,

but we are not at home, for the current is strong, and our caidjees begin to pull more vigorously, for they have a sort of superstitious dread of being on the Bosphorus after nightfall, and they give us to understand very emphatically in their broken English that they shall expect more "backshish" on their arrival than they agreed for at Tophani, pointing up to the sky and saying,—

"Plenty dark"—"No plenty sun"—"English, madama, bono chok bono"—"No bono Russe, no bono Greek"—"Turk bono, English bono; English, madama, plenty money, plenty sovereigns—caidjee chabouk home, madama, give him more shillings."

"Chabouk (make haste), then, caidjee," we reply—"sixpence more, caidjee; shudi, shudi (quick, quick)."

And now the moon rises and bathes all around in its shadowy light, and we are thankful that earth is so beautiful; and now our journey is ended—the caique touches the threshold of our "Home on the Bosphorus," Georgi and Demetri, our Greek boys, fly down to welcome us, and thus our day's shopping in Pera is ended.

## CHAPTER XV.

Difficulties attending shopping in Pera—*Sœur* Bernardine—Affection of the French troops for their *Sœurs*—More than sufficient reasons for it—A visit to *La Maison Notre Dame de la Providence*—Extraordinary scene within—Details of its arrangements—Schools connected with it—Church belonging to the Lazaristes Fathers—The orphans' dormitory—Boarding-school under the direction of the *Sœurs*—The children's chapel—A glorious panorama—Founder of the Order of the *Sœurs de la Charité*—Rules of the order—Extension of the order to other lands—Voltaire's opinion of it—Foundation of the Mission of the *Sœurs de la Charité* in Constantinople—Sweet *Sœur* Bernardine!

EVEN with our interpreter's help we still found great difficulty in shopping at Pera; especially at this juncture when we were obliged to buy so many things for the men, and did not know where to find them, as they were things out of the common way. Papafée did not always know the price; of course he never confessed his ignorance, but only shrugged his shoulders, said it was great nonsense to want them, and let the Greeks cheat as they chose.

*Sœur* Bernardine, one of the French *Sœurs de la Charité*, hearing of our difficulty, offered either to do commissions for us, or to accompany us through the streets of Pera and show us the right shops. She had been many years in the East and spoke Turkish. We availed ourselves of her kindness, and one day under her escort we traversed the streets of Galata and Pera to learn the best shops to go to: *Sœur* Bernardine knew the right price to be given for everything. She went up and down the extraordinary streets seeking for the treasures of useful, not ornamental, kind of baskets, darning cotton, and worsted stockings (the English kind of the latter are most difficult to procure in

Constantinople), gill measures too we sought and *found* with her aid, and many cooking utensils.

We procured a store of treasures in that day's shopping, and valuable information as to the shops at which to buy, and the prices to give, from *Sœur* Bernardine. As we walked along the crowded streets we met among the motley throng, as usual, many French officers and soldiers, and all drew back to let *la Sœur* pass, and taking off their hats bowed as if to a lady of noble rank; for throughout the French army exists a deep affection and gratitude to their *Sœurs*, and well may they have it towards those who have followed wherever the flag of France has gone to strife and bloodshed. Wherever her sons have lain languishing on beds of sickness, when home and friends were far, one comforter was ever at hand, one well-known form hovered by their side—*la Sœur de la Charité.*

Whenever the French armies for the last 200 years have gone out to battle, as surely as they take with them weapons of war and destruction, skilful generals to lead them to victory, gallant hearts to fight, so surely do they also take a gentle holy band of *Sœurs de la Charité;* and amid those rough soldiers and among those scenes of horror and distress the *Sœurs* move fearless and unharmed. Around them is a shield which insult dares not touch. As safe on the battle-field, or in the hospital tent, or the "ambulance" in some foreign town are they as in their convent home; the "wards of the hospital or the streets of the city are their cloisters, hired rooms are their cells, the fear of God is their grating, and a strict and holy modesty their only veil." No wonder the Frenchman pays them such respect and honour, for they are worthy of it tenfold.

After we had finished our shopping, and were very weary, *Sœur* Bernardine begged we would come and rest at their convent. *La Maison Notre Dame de la Providence* is situated in Galata, it is not far from the British and French admiralty offices, but though an extensive building and standing close to a Catholic church, it is in such a narrow, dirty little street that, unless guided there by some one knowing the way, one might wander about for an hour without discovering it. It stands in the midst of the Frank population of the city, its most filthy and abandoned haunts.

Arriving there, over a large door is written, *Maison Notre Dame de la Providence, Ecole des Sœurs de la Charité*. Raising the knocker the door opened by a pulley from within, and we entered. This convent is in itself a wonder; on one hand is the reception parlour, which is constantly thronged. Persons of all nations come here to ask information on various points; French officers come about their soldiers' wants.

Here throng the poor of all descriptions. Everybody in trouble, distress, or perplexity, seems to come here to be relieved. We pass a little further on into the great store-room, where biscuits and wine and such like articles are dispensed from this house to the "ambulances;" the ambulances are a sort of out-stations for the *Sœurs de la Charité*, established near to each hospital; a certain number of *Sœurs* under a *Supérieure* are sent to these stations, and are supplied from this convent with stores for their patients. This convent is the *Maison Mère* for all the *Sœurs* scattered about the Turkish empire; here they return when they are ill for rest and nursing. There are 100 *Sœurs* in this convent, exclusive of those sent out, and women of eight different nations are in the community.

Leaving the store-rooms we visited the schools, which contain many hundreds of children, of as many countries as are gathered together at Constantinople—which are almost all the countries of the known world—and the children of this strange gathering are all taught one common faith, gathered into one fold. It was a wonderful spectacle to look on the various faces of the little maidens, the blue-eyed German, and dark Italian; the cunning face of the Greek and stolid look of the Turk. Next to the school we passed through the courtyard, where the children play.

A door opening from this admitted us into the adjoining church, which belongs to the Lazaristes Fathers. It was very plain and possessed no ornament worthy of note, save one or two fine paintings. Ascending stairs we next visited the *Sœurs'* dispensary, which is kept in the most perfect order. The *Sœurs* are trained to make up medicines, and this is a most important branch of their work in Turkey, as they are the only doctors for large numbers of the poor, and among the poor exists a quantity of disease far exceeding any other city of the size and population of Constantinople.

Ascending another flight of stairs we came to the orphans' dormitory. This we found in beautiful order; long rows of little white beds, and at each end, curtained off, was the simple bed of a *Sœur*, who by night as well as day guarded her orphan charge. Higher still—we sighed at the number of stairs—and we found the orphans—one hundred of them, such a happy-looking set, sitting at work in a spacious room, *Sœurs* with them of course. At our request they sang a hymn. We distributed some sweetmeats among them, which gave great delight. The orphans do a great deal of needlework towards their own support; they also dress dolls in the different costumes of the country for sale, and other articles of fancy work which can be purchased in the parlour below.

The *Sœurs* have a boarding-school for

girls, of a higher rank than the day-school. There was not sufficient room for this in the convent, in consequence of the number of *Sœurs* attending the different military hospitals, and the boarding-school had been moved to a house in Pera. The *Sœurs* serve six or more military hospitals in Constantinople.

When we had seen the orphans we had not even then reached the last story; another flight yet and we found the children's chapel. It is merely a room set apart for this purpose, and tastefully ornamented, though with great simplicity. Stepping out from the chapel we found ourselves on the house-top, which forms a broad terraced walk, and—oh, what a panorama was before us—what pen could describe it? The curious maze-like streets of Constantinople lay at our feet. We were too distant to see their drawbacks, we only saw the picturesque. There was the bridge of boats, with its thronging multitudes, whose forms looked shadowy in the distance. The Golden Horn and its shipping, the distant minarets of Santa Sophia, Sultan Achmet's mosque, and many a mosque and palace, besides cypress groves, the grand seraglio, and the beautiful rounding of Seraglio point, the blue Bosphorus, the great cemetery of Scutari, the hospitals on the cliff, the Sea of Marmora, the distant chains of mountains, where the eye strives to distinguish the faint outline of Olympus. All this the eye can gather in from any eminence in Constantinople.

The *Sœurs* possessing no grounds to their house come here to catch the fresh air. Here every August the *Sœurs* make, according to their rule, a week's retreat, and those *Sœurs* from the different ambulances change and flock in here for this end, and they spend much of their time on this quiet house-top. *Sœur* Bernardine said, in her pretty broken English—

"It is the time we love the best of all, for then we come here and we have nothing to do but to pray and think of God. Last year," she said, "I was here, I was so happy, but, alas! the cholera broke out at Varna and they sent for us in haste, and I and some more had to go so quickly."

The *Sœurs de la Charité* are those whom I mentioned as having met on board the "Egyptus." They were founded two hundred years ago by St. Vincent de Paul, a man of whom it has with justice been said, he "did more good in his single life than all the *philosophers* the world ever saw." He thought that to effectually relieve the sufferings of the poor—besides the religious orders established for the relief of particular kinds of distress—there should be an order of women taken themselves from the poor, who would be thus inured to the hardships they had to endure; and he ordained that they should wear the peasant dress of the period, that they should be sent to nurse the sick at all times and in all places where they might be required as well as educate young children.

Persons wishing to enter this order were to pass five years at least in the noviciate, after which they were allowed to take the threefold vow of obedience, poverty, and chastity, but this vow was to expire every 25th of March, and to be renewed or not at the *Sœurs'* own will. No instance, we believe, has ever been recorded of a *Sœur*, after having passed through the noviciate, withdrawing. St. Vincent de Paul died in 1660, but his work lived on. He called his daughters the servants of the poor, but the people saw their deeds of love and they named them *Sœurs de la Charité.*

From France, its birthplace, this wonderful order—wonderful in its extreme simplicity—spread into all lands. They number now eleven thousand. Ladies of high rank, even princesses have laid down their rank and wealth and entered the lowly order of the daughters of St. Vincent, but the greater mass of the *Sœurs* is composed of the class for whom St. Vincent intended it—the women who in England are hospital nurses and schoolmistresses.

This is the order which made the infidel Voltaire exclaim, that if anything could make him believe in Christianity it would be such deeds as those wrought by the *Sœurs de la Charité*.

In the din of the French Revolution, even in the Reign of Terror, the *Sœurs* won respect from those fiends in human form. In the Peninsular war one town was constantly taken and retaken by the French and Spaniards. In this town was a convent of *Sœurs de la Charité*. Whichever army occupied the town they sent sentinels to guard the convent, for the influence of their gentle deeds of love triumphed over the bitter animosity of war.

The mission of *les Sœurs de la Charité* in

Constantinople was founded in the following way. Fifteen years ago a German lady came to Paris and sought to enter the order. On inquiry she was found to be above the age at which the novices are received, which is either twenty-eight or thirty. The disappointment was great, for it was the wish of her heart, and at length the superiors of the order agreed to receive her should she be willing to endure the test they would put to her. They wished to found a house in Constantinople, they said, would she go there with one companion, establish a school, and so make their footing good? She consented.

Fifteen years ago Constantinople was a very different place to Constantinople now. The Christian's life then was one, in outward things, not much unlike that of His Divine Master—pelting with stones in the street and other insults were the portion of these holy women. They persevered. *Sœur* Bernardine (for she was the lady we speak of) learnt the Turkish language, established a school—*Sœurs* came from France, and she entered their order.

Sweet *Sœur* Bernardine! my memory loves to linger upon her. We shall never meet on earth again, but never shall I forget that saintly face, or that winning, loving manner, which spoke so plainly of the well of love within her heart. The toil the *Sœurs* undergo shortens their lives; many have died of fatigue during the present war—four at the convent in Galata within a few weeks of each other. A lady who had been boarding at the convent told me she never witnessed such peaceful death-beds. Humbly but joyfully they went to Him they had so loved to serve on earth.

END OF VOL. I.